SHELLEY BOETTCHER
and DARREN OLEKSYN

2014

UNCORKED!

The Definitive Guide to
Alberta's Best Wines under $25

whitecap

Edited by: Theresa Best and Tracy Bordian
Designed by: Setareh Ashrafologhalai
Typesetting by: Jan Westendorp
Proofreading by: Eva van Emden

Many of the wine label images were provided by wineries and distributors and are
reprinted with permission. Others were photographed by the authors.

Printed in Canada

Library and Archives Canada Cataloguing in Publication
Shelley Boettcher, 1970-, author
        Uncorked! : the definitive guide to Alberta's best wines under $25 / Shelley
Boettcher and Darren Oleksyn.—Third edition.
Includes bibliographical references and index.
ISBN 978-1-77050-203-1 (pbk.)
        1. Wine and wine making—Alberta—Guidebooks. I. Oleksyn, Darren, 1968-,
author II. Title.
TP548.B63 2013   641.2'2   C2013-904090-0

The publisher acknowledges the financial support of the Government of Canada
through the Canada Book Fund (CBF) and the Province of British Columbia through
the Book Publishing Tax Credit.

13 14 15 16 17   5 4 3 2 1

CONTENTS

INTRODUCTION

You're holding in your hands a guide to buying 150 wines that each cost $25 or less, plus suggestions for wine and food pairings and more.

If you didn't already know it, this is the third edition of this book. The first—a Canadian bestseller—was released in 2010 and featured great bargains for wine lovers, available across the province of Alberta.

The third edition of the book also features fine bargains for wine lovers, available across the province. But this edition—updated from the 2012 edition—is co-written by both Shelley Boettcher and Darren Oleksyn, two friends who want to share their passion for fine wine at bargain prices with you.

What has changed since the previous editions? Vintages, and prices, too. You'll recognize a few familiar labels, but, alas, some of the previous edition's picks are now priced too high to be included. Others, for various reasons, just didn't quite make the cut this year.

But—luckily for us—there are a lot of excellent new wines available in the province, new labels that weren't for sale here in previous years.

We have chosen every wine with a metric ton of care and attention. While importers sometimes supplied wines for consideration, we don't get paid by agents for writing about their wines. Not here. Not ever. As for tasting, we mostly tasted the wines independently, in big blocks of like wines—for example, 10 or 12 Merlot wines or a dozen Sauvignon Blancs at a time. Not every wine tasted ended up in the book. Rather, we took careful notes, and then we chose the best, whittling down the lengthy list of impressive wines for sale in our market. In particular, we looked for top-notch value-priced wines that represent a range of regions, countries, styles and grapes.

Keep in mind that vintages will change as stock sells out at certain stores, but don't worry if you find a different vintage of the same wine; while wines certainly vary from year to year, most of these producers are consistently reliable every vintage.

And although we verified all prices at press time, they may not always be exact. Alberta's liquor market is privatized, which means retailers don't have to charge the same at every store. A $22 bottle at one store may be $17 or, for that matter, $28 at another; shop around and compare.

Still, you get the idea. This book is loaded with dozens of delicious wines at bargain prices. Buy a bottle or two or ten. Buy a case or two or ten. Taste your way through the world's wine regions, bargain by bargain. Cheers!

—Shelley and Darren

HOW TO USE THIS BOOK

How should you read this book? Read it from start to finish, if that's your style. If you know you're a wine geek, pick and choose, based on your favourite grapes, regions or producers. Browse by price. Explore the wine-producing world, country by country or grape by grape. Choose wines for a certain occasion, casual Fridays, grandma's birthday, New Year's Eve or a family barbecue—we've listed suggestions for each wine under the "Uncork" heading. Or you can just admire the lovely labels.

Each wine listing has this information at the top:

- A listing title (the big, bold text at the top left of each page): Usually but not always, this is the most prominent piece of information on the label. Some wines have no particular name; in these cases, we have listed the wine by the name of the winery, or by the winery and the series, or by the winery and the variety—we're trying to help you find the wine as easily as possible in the store.
- Winery: The company that makes the wine.
- Wine name: The moniker that sets this wine apart from other wines made by the same winery or, for that matter, by anyone else.
- Variety or Type: In the first part of the book (the red wine, white wine and rosé sections), "Variety" is the type of grape used to make the wine—for example, Cabernet Sauvignon, Sauvignon Blanc, Pinot Noir. In the second part of the book (Bargain Bubbles and Sweet & Fortified Wines), "Type" is the style of wine—for example, Prosecco (a sparkling wine made in Italy), cava (a sparkling wine made in Spain), port (a sweet wine made in Portugal).
- Year: This date—usually called the "vintage"—is the year the grapes were harvested. A "Non-vintage" wine is a blend of wines made in different years.
- Origin: The place the wine comes from, which may include a legally designated appellation and/or region.
- Price: The cost of the wine. You probably figured that out yourself.

The closure each wine uses is shown with an icon:

 Regular cork

 Screw cap

 Sparkling wine cork

TEN TIPS ON CELLARING YOUR WINE

1. **Keep wine out of the kitchen (unless you're opening it).** Corkscrews? Yes. Wine? No. Your kitchen is too warm (and probably too busy). It's not the best place in which to store wine properly.

2. **Store your wine in the coolest part of your house.** Under the spare-bedroom bed or in a spare closet will work if you don't have a basement or room for a wine fridge.

3. **Garages are for cars, not cuvées.** Unless your garage is heated, it's too cold in the winter. You'll freeze everything. And your wine can pick up icky smells like car exhaust or mice or just plain ol' dust. Your garage is for empties—until you ship 'em off to a grateful Boy Scout or cash 'em in for money to buy a few new vintages.

4. **Tip 'em over. Gently.** They're not bowling pins. Lay your bottles gently on their sides so their corks touch the wine at all times. (Not a big deal if you mostly have screw caps.)

5. **Turn off the lights.** Keep the room dark. Too much light will fade your pretty labels and oxidize the wines.

6. **Stay away from the cat box, the dog bed, mothballs and oil paints.** Strong smells will seep into your wines. Cat pee may be a desirable odour in some Sauvignon Blanc wines (I'm serious), but let the winemaker decide that. Not you. Or your cat.

7. **Jiggle elsewhere.** Above your washing machine? Or beside your treadmill? Not good. The vibration can damage the corks.

8. **Get wet.** Humidity keeps corks from drying out, and in the cold, dry climate of Alberta, that's important. If you can't afford a humidifier, put a bucket or two of water in your "cellar." The moisture will help maintain good humidity.

9. **Planning to buy a wine fridge? Consider size and noise.** How many bottles do you plan to keep at one time? Does the unit have racks that will fit whatever it is that you prefer to drink? How loud is it when it runs?

10. **Money's no object? Then shop.** Hire a professional. Myriad companies out there will build professional cellars with humidity and temperature controls. Shop around. Ask friends and restaurant staff. Google.

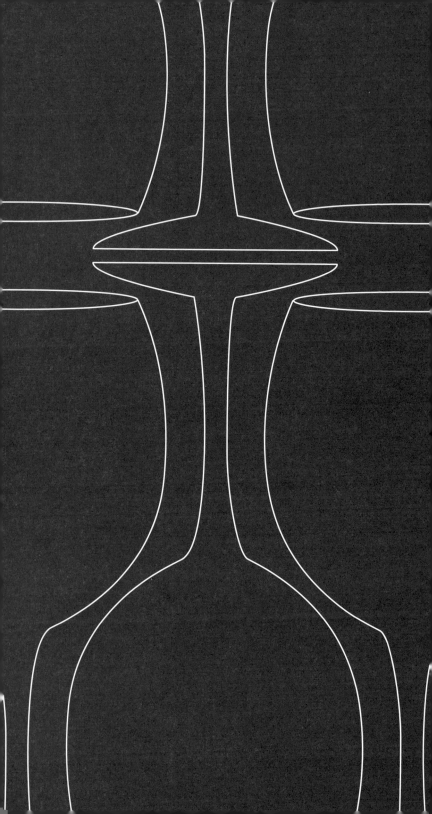

FIRST, THE RED WINES

1884

Bodegas Escorihuela Gascón	1884 Reservado
WINERY	WINE NAME
Cabernet Sauvignon	2011
VARIETY	YEAR
Mendoza, Argentina	$14
ORIGIN	PRICE

CLOSURE

Looking for something to grab quickly on your way to a party? Full-bodied and easy-drinking is always popular. Be a hero and take this Argentine Cabernet Sauvignon. It's loaded with blackcurrant, vanilla, mocha, plum, spice and leather. The nice balance, longish finish and supple tannins should be crowd-pleasers. And at just $14, you could buy two bottles. Hero indeed.

The name "1884" refers to the year that winery founder Don Miguel Escorihuela

Gascón planted vineyards in Mendoza after coming to Argentina from Aragon, Spain.

TRIVIA The winemaking team is nuts about polo. In fact, a polo ground was built near one of the vineyards, and every year the winery gathers amateur players to mount up and face some of Argentina's best teams.

PAIR WITH Argentine barbecue, grilled ribs, hard cheeses.

UNCORK When you're trying to impress a wine snob (you don't have to reveal the price).

ALTOS LAS HORMIGAS

Altos Las Hormigas	Clasîco	
WINERY	WINE NAME	
Malbec	2012	
VARIETY	YEAR	
Mendoza, Argentina	$17	
ORIGIN	PRICE	CLOSURE

Altos Las Hormigas was created in 1995 when Italian winemaker Alberto Antonini and entrepreneur and wine lover Antonio Morescalchi visited Argentina, checking out the prospects for investment. They were impressed, and they quickly purchased 216 hectares of vineyards in the Mendoza area and started making stellar wines like this Malbec. There's lots of smoke and spice on the nose, with flavours of blueberry, blackberry, plum, earth, vanilla and iron on a moderately tannic finish.

TRIVIA "Altos Las Hormigas" translates to "ant heights." When the vineyards were planted, the team discovered millions of ants, which started attacking the young vine shoots. Rather than killing the insects, the owners found ways to distract them away from the vines until the plants were stronger. They then decided to name the winery after those pesky ants.

PAIR WITH Burgers, ribs and sausages, hearty stews, lamb.

UNCORK Sunday dinners, post-rodeo relaxing, family gatherings.

CATENA

Bodega Catena Zapata	Catena	
WINERY	WINE NAME	
Cabernet Sauvignon	2010	
VARIETY	YEAR	
Mendoza, Argentina	$18	
ORIGIN	PRICE	CLOSURE

Viña Catena Zapata has been one of the leaders of high-altitude grape-growing in Argentina for years. The grapes for this wine come from altitudes of 1,000 metres above sea level or higher, roughly the same altitude as Calgary. High altitudes allow the grapes to get plenty of sunshine during the day while enjoying cool nights that let the grapes rest, keeping the acid levels high and the flavours fresh. Blackberry, violet, plum,

mint, tobacco and black licorice are just some of the flavours you'll find in this dependable Cabernet Sauvignon.

TRIVIA In 2012, Nicolás Catena received *Wine Spectator* magazine's Distinguished Service Award for his leadership in Argentina's wine industry.

PAIR WITH Veal tenderloin, grilled game, pasta and meat sauce.

UNCORK While watching soccer, after a day of hiking or skiing in the Rockies. Or age it a few years.

FABRE MONTMAYOU

Fabre Montmayou Winery and Vineyards	Gran Reserva
WINERY	WINE NAME
Malbec	2009
VARIETY	YEAR
Mendoza, Argentina	$25
ORIGIN	PRICE

CLOSURE

Fabre Montmayou was started by Hervé Joyaux Fabre, who was born to a family of wine *négociants* (merchants), in Bordeaux, France. Fabre came to Argentina in the 1990s with the dream of starting his own winery. He started buying vineyards—some that were planted in 1904—and his dream took flight. Notes of violets, mint, plum, blackberries and licorice soar out of the glass from this well-balanced beauty.

TRIVIA A *négociant* is a person who gathers wine, grapes or grape juice from producers and sells the already completed wine as is, makes his or her own wine, or blends wines before selling them.

PAIR WITH Argentine churrasco (grilled meats), veal cutlets, lamb kebabs, aged cheeses.

UNCORK Watching hockey on TV, summer barbecues, tailgate parties, guys' nights.

FELINO

Viña Cobos	Felino
WINERY	WINE NAME
Malbec	2011
VARIETY	YEAR
Mendoza, Argentina	$20
ORIGIN	PRICE

CLOSURE

UNCORKED!

Viña Cobos is a joint-venture winery combining the talents of American winemaker Paul Hobbs and the Argentine husband-and-wife team of Luis Barraud and Andrea Marchiori. They produce four lines of wines, with Cobos being the entry level. There's plenty of jammy fruit in this Malbec, including blackberry, blueberry and plum, plus violet notes. It's a great introduction to the refined, yet powerful, wines made by Hobbs.

TRIVIA The label for the Felino wines features a piece of Argentine Aboriginal art.

PAIR WITH Filet mignon with a cherry wine reduction, hard cheeses, roast pork.

UNCORK First dates, hockey nights with the guys, anniversary dinners.

KAIKEN

Kaiken		
WINERY		

Malbec	2010	
VARIETY	YEAR	

Mendoza, Argentina	$14	
ORIGIN	PRICE	CLOSURE

The folks behind a Chilean winery—Montes Premium Wines—started Kaiken. The move into Argentina is symbolized on the Kaiken label, which features the Andes mountains that separate Argentina and Chile. In fact, a Kaiken is a wild goose that flies between the neighbouring countries.

You'll find great value from this rich, concentrated wine with supple tannins and outstanding balance. Expect flavours and aromas of blueberry, blackberry, earth, vanilla, spice and leather.

TRIVIA The big mountain in the middle of the label represents Aconcagua, the highest peak in the Americas at just over 6,960 metres (22,834 feet) above sea level. Canada's highest spot is the top of Yukon's Mount Logan, 5,959 metres (19,551 feet) above sea level.

PAIR WITH Grilled sausages, bison burgers, steak, wild game.

UNCORK Dinner with your boss or your date's parents, watching Argentine soccer star Lionel Messi, after a day of hiking.

LLAMA

Belasco de Baquedano	Llama
WINERY	WINE NAME
Malbec	2011
VARIETY	YEAR
Alto Agrelo Valley, Lujan de Cuyo, Mendoza, Argentina	$17
ORIGIN	PRICE

CLOSURE

Like its namesake pack animal, this wine can carry a load, pleasing lots of people. Using grapes from vines more than 100 years old, it features notes of blackberry, black cherry and blueberry plus leather, vanilla and spice. If you want to tune up your sniffer before you taste, you can visit the "aroma hall" at the Belasco de Baquedano winery. The hall is a room with 46 stations where you push different buttons to release different scents, many of which can be found in the winery's Malbecs.

TRIVIA Farmers in North America occasionally use llamas to protect their livestock, often sheep, from predators such as coyotes.

PAIR WITH Juicy grilled steaks, bison, beef bourguignon.

UNCORK Weekday dinners, block parties, campfires on the beach.

SANTA JULIA

Bodega Santa Julia	Santa Julia	
WINERY	WINE NAME	
Malbec	2011	
VARIETY	YEAR	
Mendoza, Argentina	$12	
ORIGIN	PRICE	CLOSURE

One of Mendoza's largest wine producers, Familia Zuccardi (literally, the Zuccardi family), is behind Bodega Santa Julia. With ancestral roots that date back to Italy, Alberto Zuccardi, an engineer, planted the family's first vineyard in the 1960s partly to show off a fancy irrigation system he had created. (Mendoza doesn't get much rain, so water management is very important.) His son, José Alberto, joined the enterprise in the 1980s and then named the winery after his only daughter, Julia, who now manages the

winery's restaurant, which specializes in Argentine *parrilla* (barbecue). The full-bodied, dark purple–red wine is a real tooth-stainer, with ripe, dark plummy notes, smooth tannins and a nice long finish.

TRIVIA Malbec is a thin-skinned grape that has its roots in France, but excels in Argentina.

PAIR WITH Anything big and meaty—steaks, ribs, burgers, venison.

UNCORK Family reunions, barbecues, Saturday afternoons on the patio.

FIRST, THE RED WINES

TERRAZAS DE LOS ANDES

Terrazas de los Andes	Reserva
WINERY	WINE NAME
Cabernet Sauvignon	2009
VARIETY	YEAR
Mendoza, Argentina	$18
ORIGIN	PRICE	CLOSURE

Located on the eastern side of the Andes, Mendoza is the largest wine-producing region in South America. While Terrazas de los Andes made its mark internationally for its Malbec wines, the winery produces many beautiful wines. Take this Cabernet Sauvignon, for one. If you like chocolate, this may be the wine for you. Toasty mocha aromas are complemented by blackberry, plum and mint. On the palate you'll find blackberry, black cherry, vanilla, plum and earth.

TRIVIA Terrazas de los Andes is owned by LVMH Moët Hennessy, a luxury brand company with holdings that include Louis Vuitton handbags—not just good wine.

PAIR WITH Beef stew, pulled pork sandwiches, roast meats.

UNCORK Dinner with the boss, frosty winter evenings. Or cellar it for a few years.

TIERRA SECRETA

Bodegas Tierra Secreta	Tierra Secreta	
WINERY	WINE NAME	
Malbec	2010	
VARIETY	YEAR	
Mendoza, Argentina	$18	
ORIGIN	PRICE	CLOSURE

Argentina could be called Malbec's "secret earth" (the English translation for "Tierra Secreta"). A second-tier grape in its homeland of France, Malbec has become a huge star in Argentina—and the rest of the wine-drinking world, too. It's easy to see why. Just try this deep-purple sipper with flavours of blackberry, toast, vanilla, blueberry and chopped herbs. Full-bodied, but with soft tannins, it's a natural crowd-pleaser.

TRIVIA A wine glass made specifically for Malbec was unveiled on April 17, 2013, which happens to be Malbec World Day. The glass was developed by the Riedel company, which makes special glasses for pretty much every grape out there.

PAIR WITH Chili con carne, sweet potato quesadillas, grilled meats.

UNCORK Malbec World Day, or any day that ends in "y" for that matter.

FIRST, THE RED WINES

FAITH

St Hallett Wines	Faith	
WINERY	WINE NAME	

Shiraz	2010	
VARIETY	YEAR	

Barossa Valley, Australia	$20	
ORIGIN	PRICE	CLOSURE

This wine has appeared in all three editions of *Uncorked!* Australian Shiraz at its finest—juicy and jammy, with hints of blackberry and cherries—this is a wine for anyone who needs faith, whether it's believing in something, in someone or simply in the power of a rich, big, powerful red wine.

The winery is named after a long-ago Australian surveyor. As for the "saint" part of his name? No one knows.

TRIVIA We know Shiraz as wine (and a grape). Hafíz of Shiraz was a 14th-century Sufi poet who wrote about love, faith and drinking too much wine.

PAIR WITH Sausages or steak. Or just enjoy by itself.

UNCORK Family gatherings or any time someone says "bring a red" but doesn't tell you what's on the menu.

HUGO

Hugo Wines	Hugo
WINERY	WINE NAME
Shiraz	2009
VARIETY	YEAR
McLaren Vale, Australia	$22
ORIGIN	PRICE

CLOSURE

Hugo Wines is located in a small Australian town called McLaren Flat, population 600, give or take a few. The Hugo family started growing some of the grapes for this winery in 1950, and almost 65 years later, they still work that same land. They have a range of wines, including Grenache, Sauvignon Blanc, Chardonnay and Cabernet Sauvignon, but it's the Shiraz that we're focusing on here. Indeed, more than 50 percent of the grapes

grown in McLaren Vale are Shiraz. This isn't your over-the-top jam-bomb Oz red, however. The Hugo take on the famous wine is much more elegant and subdued, with notes of blackberry, pepper and mocha.

TRIVIA The name "Hugo" likely comes from a German word for "heart, mind and spirit"; in 2011, it was ranked 439 in the top 1,000 baby names in the US.

PAIR WITH Grilled Italian sausages, steak. Or just enjoy by itself.

UNCORK Birthdays, camping trips, family reunions, barbecues.

KOONUNGA HILL

Penfolds	Koonunga Hill	
WINERY	WINE NAME	
Shiraz/Cabernet Sauvignon	2010	
VARIETY	YEAR	
South Australia, Australia	$18	
ORIGIN	PRICE	CLOSURE

One of Australia's most famous wineries, Penfolds is known among hardcore wine lovers for its Grange—a big, complex red wine that ages beautifully and, well, costs a lot. The Koonunga Hill line of wines is much easier to find and easier on the pocketbook. It's a classic Australian red with rich and refined fruits including blackberry, blueberry and cherry, with hints of vanilla and white pepper.

TRIVIA Penfolds's chief winemaker, Peter Gago, has myriad celebrity friends and fans, including Tool frontman (and Arizona winemaker) Maynard James Keenan, Diana Krall and Elvis Costello, and Lance Armstrong.

PAIR WITH Burgers, sausages, hearty stews.

UNCORK Tuesday nights, weekend hockey or football games, après-ski relaxing by the fireplace.

TERRA BAROSSA

Thorn-Clarke Wines	Terra Barossa	
WINERY	WINE NAME	
Shiraz	2010	
VARIETY	YEAR	
Barossa Valley, Australia	$19	
ORIGIN	PRICE	CLOSURE

Many Thorns and Clarkes work together at this winery. Owned by David and Cheryl (née Thorn) Clark, the estate is managed by their son Sam. Cheryl's brother, also named David, manages some of the vineyards, and her father, Ron Thorn, owns and manages one of Australia's oldest Shiraz vineyards—likely even one of the oldest in the world (it was around in 1854, maybe even earlier). A mere baby by comparison, this dark purple–red

wine is loaded with yummy plum and vanilla notes. Very smooth, rich and easy to drink.

TRIVIA The Barossa Valley was mostly settled by German immigrants in the early 1800s; over time, subsequent generations created their own German dialect, now referred to by linguists as "Barossa German."

PAIR WITH Roast turkey, anything big and meaty such as roast lamb or Italian sausages. Or just enjoy by itself.

UNCORK With your favourite elders, long-time friends, Barossa Germans, or at Thanksgiving or Christmas dinner.

FIRST, THE RED WINES

THREE GARDENS

Langmeil Winery	Three Gardens
WINERY	WINE NAME
Shiraz/Grenache/Mataro	2010
VARIETY	YEAR
Barossa Valley, Australia	$23
ORIGIN	PRICE · CLOSURE

When you go to a winery and see the big stainless-steel tanks and rooms filled with barrels, it all seems very high-tech. But really at the core of everything, the wine industry is about farming. It's hard to make good wine without good grapes. At Langmeil they look at their vineyards as gardens, lending a more hands-on feel. This wine is from three different vineyards, er, gardens. The letters SGM stand for the grape varieties used in the blend—Shiraz, Grenache and Mataro (the Aussie name for Mourvèdre). A robust wine

with aging potential, it has sour cherry, black raspberry, blackberry, violet, spice, iron, and mint flavours and aromas.

TRIVIA One Langmeil vineyard in Australia's Barossa Valley holds some of the oldest grapevines in the world. The Freedom 1843 vineyard was indeed planted in 1843. In the Barossa, vines that old aren't just known as old vines; they're called "ancestor vines."

PAIR WITH Braised lamb shanks, duck confit, wild game, meaty pizzas.

UNCORK Break open your SGM while you're watching *CSI* on CTV.

WIRRA WIRRA

Wirra Wirra Vineyards	Scrubby Rise
WINERY	WINE NAME
Red blend (see below)	2010
VARIETY	YEAR
Adelaide, Australia	$16
ORIGIN	PRICE	CLOSURE

Wirra Wirra founder Greg Trott, who started Wirra Wirra by rebuilding a derelict winery in Australia's Adelaide region, was a creative thinker. Trott, who passed away in 2005, had plans to build a working catapult, though he never reached that goal. He did, however, construct a heavy-duty wooden fence at the winery's entrance that's estimated to weigh 10 tons. This is a pretty heavy blend of Shiraz, Cabernet Sauvignon and Petit Verdot, with leather, tobacco, currant, raspberry and black cherry flavours.

TRIVIA The Scrubby Rise vineyard, which produces the grapes for this wine, was actually a flat, barren land before it was planted with vines. But that didn't stop Greg Trott from giving it a more evocative name.

PAIR WITH Sausages, burgers, roast duck.

UNCORK Kitchen parties, Saturday barbecues, block parties.

FIRST, THE RED WINES

2010 Shiraz
Cabernet Petit Verdot from Adelaide
SCRUBBY RISE
WIRRA WIRRA

ZVY-GELT

Weingut Meinhard Forstreiter	Zvy-Gelt	
WINERY	WINE NAME	
Zweigelt	2009	
VARIETY	YEAR	
Lower Austria, Austria	$16	
ORIGIN	PRICE	CLOSURE

The folks at Meinhard Forstreiter had wine lovers in mind when they named this bright and peppy red wine. The name "Zvy-Gelt" is the phonetic spelling for the grape, Zweigelt, used in this wine from Austria. If you like Pinot Noir or Gamay, give this a try. It's light, fresh and zippy, with soft tannins and flavours of cherry, raspberry, cranberry, vanilla and peppery spice. A great summer red that would pair well with a variety of foods. Now if only someone would make a phonetic label for Agiorgitiko.

TRIVIA The label for this wine is very similar to the cover of British band Franz Ferdinand's second album, *You Could Have It So Much Better.* The true inspiration for both, though, is a 1920s poster by Russian artist Alexander Rodchenko.

PAIR WITH Pizza, pasta puttanesca, Hungarian goulash.

UNCORK Summer picnics, weekday dinners, beach parties, camping trips. Serve slightly chilled.

BLUE MOUNTAIN

Blue Mountain Vineyard and Cellars
....
WINERY

Gamay Noir	2011
VARIETY	YEAR

Okanagan Valley, BC, Canada	$25	
ORIGIN	PRICE	CLOSURE

Different vintages of this wine have appeared in all three editions of *Uncorked!* Located near the small town of Okanagan Falls—known by the locals as OK Falls—Blue Mountain is owned by the Mavety family, who started their wine journey by growing grapes for other people before setting up their own gig in 1991. The Mavetys produce a portfolio of wines from grapes suited to the climate on their estate vineyard, everything from Chardonnay to Pinot Noir, to outstanding sparkling wines, to this Gamay Noir, which offers flavours of plum, black raspberry, black cherry and spice.

TRIVIA Gamay Noir is an ancient grape used to make France's Beaujolais wines. The earliest recorded mention of it dates back to the 1300s—in France, that is, not the Okanagan.

PAIR WITH Roast chicken, turkey, veal, ham, salmon.

UNCORK Family reunions, Sunday dinners, Thanksgiving dinners, first dates.

FIRST, THE RED WINES

INNISKILLIN

Inniskillin Okanagan Estate	Inniskillin	
WINERY	WINE NAME	
Cabernet Sauvignon	2011	
VARIETY	YEAR	
Okanagan Valley, BC, Canada	$20	
ORIGIN	PRICE	CLOSURE

Inniskillin is one of Canada's most historic wineries. It was founded in Niagara, Ontario, in 1975, the first winery to get a licence in Canada since 1929. Thanks to the pioneering work of Donald Ziraldo and Karl Kaiser, Inniskillin helped put Canada on the wine map, especially for its renowned icewines. In 1994, the company started another winery in the Okanagan Valley, and that's where this well-rounded, medium-bodied Cabernet Sauvignon comes from. Twist off the screw

cap and you'll discover raspberry, blackberry, tobacco leaf, toast, vanilla and plum flavours.

TRIVIA The Inniskillin name is based on a former regiment of the British Army, the Royal Inniskilling Dragoons, who fought in the area during the War of 1812.

PAIR WITH Hamburgers, chicken burgers, sausages or lamb souvlaki.

UNCORK Watching the Winter Olympic Games, Sunday afternoons reading by the fireplace, steak nights.

NK'MIP

Nk'Mip Cellars	Talon	
WINERY	WINE NAME	
Red blend (see below)	2011	
VARIETY	YEAR	
Okanagan Valley, BC, Canada	$25	
ORIGIN	PRICE	CLOSURE

Nk'Mip is the first Aboriginal-owned winery in North America. The Osoyoos Indian Band, which shares ownership with Constellation Brands, is one of the biggest vineyard holders in the valley. Named in honour of the thunderbird, an important symbol in Aboriginal culture, this new wine is a juicy, medium-full-bodied blend of Cabernet Sauvignon, Syrah, Cabernet Franc, Merlot, Malbec and Pinot Noir. Expect plum, black licorice, blackcurrant, blueberry and vanilla notes.

TRIVIA Thunderbirds are mythological creatures that symbolize power and strength; their wings are said to create thunder as they fly.

PAIR WITH Steak, wild game, roasted meats, stews.

UNCORK Canada Day celebrations, friends' parties, weekend dinners, to cap off a day of bird-watching.

FIRST, THE RED WINES

RED ROOSTER

Red Rooster Winery	Cabernet Merlot
WINERY	WINE NAME
Red blend (see below)	2010
VARIETY	YEAR
Okanagan Valley, BC, Canada	$18
ORIGIN	PRICE
	CLOSURE

Since 1997, the team at Red Rooster has been creating wines to crow about. There's definitely a rooster theme going on: the name for their seasonal patio grill is The Pecking Room. The winery is filled with art, both permanent installations (a naked guy with a suitcase) and temporary displays. Visitors can also register for a primer on wine-tasting lingo so they can look like pros when they swirl and sip. This Cabernet Merlot is certainly worth trying. Made predominantly of

Cabernet Franc and Merlot, with a bit of Cabernet Sauvignon and Malbec for good measure, it boasts plum, tobacco leaf, leather, sour cherry, redcurrant and toast flavours.

TRIVIA Fans of Red Rooster's wines can get an up-close view of vineyard life by adopting a row of vines at the Naramata winery. A sign identifies each person's row in the vineyard, and "parents" also receive a certificate of adoption, discounts on gift purchases, a newsletter and a case of wine. If they want, "parents" can also help with the harvest. The program is so popular, there's a waiting list.

PAIR WITH Meaty pizzas, baked ham, veal scaloppini, barbecued chicken.

UNCORK After a day at the farmers' market, tailgate parties, Saturday nights at the neighbour's house.

120

Santa Rita	120	
WINERY	WINE NAME	
Cabernet Sauvignon	2011	
VARIETY	YEAR	
Central Valley, Chile	$12	
ORIGIN	PRICE	CLOSURE

The Santa Rita winery was born in 1880, started by Domingo Fernandez in Alto Jahuel, Chile. Throughout its long history, Santa Rita has built a reputation for producing both reliable everyday wines and expensive, limited-production wines. The 120 line falls into the former category. The name honours the 120 freedom fighters who, the story goes, took refuge on the property where the winery now stands during the Chilean War of Independence in the early 1800s. You can enjoy a respite from a stressful day with a glass of this soft, supple red with flavours of cassis, blackcurrant, blackberry, vanilla and leather.

TRIVIA Chile is about 4,000 kilometres (2,500 miles) long, but only an average of 150 kilometres (95 miles) wide, the distance from Calgary to Red Deer. The capital of Chile, Santiago, is actually further east than New York City. That question was a stumper in Trivial Pursuit. Now you know.

PAIR WITH Roast chicken, meat loaf, grilled bratwurst, pepperoni pizza.

UNCORK On September 18, Chile's Independence Day, or any weekday when you want a little pick-me-up and don't want to break the bank.

FIRST, THE RED WINES

CLAVA

Viña Quintay	Clava Coastal Reserve
WINERY	WINE NAME
Pinot Noir	2010
VARIETY	YEAR
Casablanca Valley, Chile	$16
ORIGIN	PRICE	CLOSURE

"Quintay" means "go with the flow" in the native tongue of this area of Chile. What an apt name for this wine from the Casablanca Valley, a cooler part of the country that is drawing attention from the international wine crowd. This Pinot Noir isn't stuck on titles, finite vineyard plots and fancy terroir—leave that to Burgundy. Instead it's an unpretentious wine that puts smiles on peoples' faces. With delicate fruit flavours like strawberry, cherry and raspberry, it's a great wine for sitting back and going with the flow.

TRIVIA A *clava* is a polished stone shield or sceptre used by Chilean chiefs about 500 years ago. You can see one on the label for this wine.

PAIR WITH Pork tenderloin, roast chicken or turkey, grilled cheese sandwiches.

UNCORK Weekday dinners, block parties, game nights, bridal showers.

KOYLE

Viña Koyle	Reserva
WINERY	WINE NAME
Cabernet Sauvignon	2010
VARIETY	YEAR
Alto Colchagua, Chile	$17
ORIGIN	PRICE

CLOSURE

It's hard to go wrong with Chilean Cabernet Sauvignon if you're looking for a crowd-pleasing red. This one comes from the Undurraga family, one of Chile's legendary wine dynasties with six generations of winemaking under their belt. Although Viña Undurraga is still in existence (there's more about the winery on page 32), the actual Undurraga family now owns Koyle. When you pop this cork, you'll be greeted by aromas of blackberry, plum, vanilla and black licorice.

They carry over to the palate, with blackcurrant, cassis and cedar joining the party.

TRIVIA "Koyle" is the name of an endangered plant that grows in Chile; it has beautiful purple flowers and grows in the winery's mountain vineyards.

PAIR WITH Steak, roast beef, game, gourmet burgers.

UNCORK When you're asked to bring a red wine, but you don't know what's on the menu, weekend barbecues, winter evenings.

FIRST, THE RED WINES

MARQUES DE CASA CONCHA

Concha y Toro	Marques de Casa Concha	
WINERY	WINE NAME	

Cabernet Sauvignon	2010	
VARIETY	YEAR	

Puente Alto, Chile	$20	
ORIGIN	PRICE	CLOSURE

UNCORKED!

The Marques de Casa Concha was a noble title handed out by the Spanish king in the 1700s. Winery founder Don Melchor de Santiago Concha y Toro was the seventh Marques de Casa Concha; he started the winery in 1993, and brought back grape vines from France to establish the vineyards. (The red named in his honour, Don Melchor, is considered to be one of Chile's best wines, vintage after vintage, but, alas, it's too expensive to include here.)

As for this noble wine, it's a bit of a bruiser. Beneath the firm tannins and zesty acid of this full-bodied wine you'll find blackberry, mint, blackcurrant and plum.

TRIVIA Concha y Toro is a sponsor of Manchester United, perhaps the most famous soccer (some call it football) team in the world.

PAIR WITH Braised meats, Chateaubriand for two, hard cheeses like manchego.

UNCORK Anniversary dinners, or when you're going to meet "the parents" for the first time. Decant or age for a few years.

MONTES ALPHA

Montes Wines	Montes Alpha	
WINERY	WINE NAME	
Merlot/Carménère	2010	
VARIETY	YEAR	
Colchagua Valley, Chile	$25	
ORIGIN	PRICE	CLOSURE

Aurelio Montes was a 10-year-old city kid when he made up his mind he wanted to live on a ranch. Eventually, he discovered wine and became a winemaker. He was 39 and a father of five kids when he started the Montes winery at the urging of his wife, who believed in his dream. Now it's one of South America's most famous wineries, with myriad labels and vineyards in Chile and Argentina, and a slew of wonderful wines such as this one. This medium-bodied Merlot blend can

likely be aged for a few years, or you can simply enjoy its minty, raspberry, cherry, pepper notes now.

TRIVIA Alpha is the first letter of the Greek alphabet, what we now call A; it's also a term used to describe the dominant person or animal (or, in this case, wine!) in a group.

PAIR WITH A nice, juicy steak, hard aged cheddar or Parmigiano Reggiano, chicken souvlaki.

UNCORK Steak night, Sunday dinner, Friday night unwinding.

SIBARIS

Viña Undurraga	Sibaris Reserva Especial	
WINERY	WINE NAME	
Pinot Noir	2012	
VARIETY	YEAR	
Maipo Valley, Chile	$15	
ORIGIN	PRICE	CLOSURE

UNCORKED!

Viña Undurraga's history dates back to the late 1800s, when Francisco Undurraga Vicuña brought Cabernet Sauvignon and Pinot Noir clippings from France, as well as young Riesling and Gewürztraminer vines from Germany. This lovely Pinot proves the long journey was worthwhile. There's a lot of depth here, with the flavours and aromas including tea, spice, currant, cherry, cranberry, raspberry, vanilla and a bit of barnyard.

TRIVIA In 1903, Viña Undurraga became the first Chilean winery to export to the US, delivering a case of Pinot Noir to each of the 45 states that existed at the time.

PAIR WITH Wild mushroom ragout, pork tenderloin with truffle sauce, Mediterranean vegetables, roast chicken.

UNCORK Anniversary dinners, wedding parties, Thanksgiving, Christmas.

VITRAL

Viña Maipo	Vitral Reserva
WINERY	WINE NAME
Cabernet Sauvignon	2011
VARIETY	YEAR
Maipo Valley, Chile	$17
ORIGIN	PRICE	CLOSURE

Viña Maipo was started in 1948 in the legendary Maipo Valley, Chile's best-known wine region; it's now owned by Concha y Toro, another iconic Chilean brand. Just south of Santiago—the country's capital—the vineyards are planted in the Andes foothills. While the winery also makes white wines, the team is especially renowned for their reds. This easy-drinking, fruit-forward Cabernet Sauvignon is deep purple, with a long finish, supple tannins and flavours of blackberry, plum, licorice, vanilla and mint.

TRIVIA Every December 8, villagers in the town of Maipo hold a procession in honour of the Virgin Mary and then gather at the church to pray for successful crops.

PAIR WITH Rosemary roasted potatoes and lamb shanks, prime rib.

UNCORK Family dinners, hanging out with the guys, Grey Cups and Super Bowls.

BEAUJOLAIS-VILLAGES

Maison Joseph Drouhin	Beaujolais-Villages	
WINERY	WINE NAME	
Gamay	2011	
VARIETY	YEAR	
Beaujolais-Villages, France	$16	
ORIGIN	PRICE	CLOSURE

Gamay is the grape here, an ancient grape used in making France's famous Beaujolais wines; indeed, the earliest recorded mention of it dates back to the 1300s. Gamay is a good red for white fans to try because it is light-bodied and gentle, not big and bossy as so many reds can be. While you can find both Beaujolais and Beaujolais-Villages wines in stores, the term "Villages" simply refers to a handful of towns that produce exceptional Beaujolais, according to the wine laws of the French government. Maison Joseph Drouhin

is one of the best-known Beaujolais producers, so perhaps not surprisingly, this one is classic, with flavours of strawberry, raspberry and Twizzlers Nibs, spicy and with lots of fresh acidity.

TRIVIA The third Thursday of every November is Beaujolais Nouveau day, a special day marked internationally by the release of the latest vintage of a very young style of Beaujolais.

PAIR WITH Tuna steak, salmon, roast chicken or turkey.

UNCORK Now, at picnics, casual Fridays, Sunday afternoon lunches.

BILA-HAUT

M. Chapoutier	Les Vignes de Bila-Haut
WINERY	WINE NAME
Syrah/Grenache/Carignan	2011
VARIETY	YEAR
Côtes du Roussillon Villages, France	$14
ORIGIN	PRICE	CLOSURE

A different vintage of this wine appeared in the 2013 edition of *Uncorked!* The Chapoutier family motto is "do and hope"—appropriate, really, for a family of winemakers. They're obviously doing something right—they've had vineyards in France since 1808, and M. Chapoutier is easily one of France's best-known wineries.

Michel Chapoutier is the man at the helm of the winery, which has vineyards across the country. This red blend is overflowing with dark, ripe fruit notes, including blackberry,

black cherry and blueberry. It also has notes of iron, hoisin sauce and licorice.

TRIVIA M. Chapoutier puts Braille on all of its labels. Michel Chapoutier started the process after a blind musician friend said how difficult it was to choose wine when you're visually impaired. The company now financially supports projects around the world for people who are visually impaired.

PAIR WITH Lamb dishes, sausages, venison, steak.

UNCORK Now, with Francophiles, or at large family gatherings.

FIRST, THE RED WINES

CHAMPY

Maison Champy	Bourgogne Pinot Noir
WINERY	WINE NAME
Pinot Noir	2011
VARIETY	YEAR
Burgundy, France	$20
ORIGIN	PRICE

CLOSURE

Maison Champy, established in 1720, has one of the longest histories in Burgundy. In 1990, Pierre Meurgey, his father Henri, and a group of shareholders bought Champy. Meurgey and winemaker/friend Dimitri Bazas are focused on producing wines of purity and balance. This Pinot Noir is perfectly balanced, with aromas of baking spices such as nutmeg and cinnamon, plus cherry, vanilla and cranberry. On the palate, there are also notes of cherry, raspberry, spice and tea.

TRIVIA Champy produced 30,000 bottles of this wine in 2011. About a quarter of them have screw caps. The rest were closed with corks. The screw cap wines are meant for North America, while the corks are aimed at the European market. (Some bottles with corks have made their way into Alberta this year. If it's a big deal to you, shop around.)

PAIR WITH Duck, lamb souvlaki, mushroom risotto.

UNCORK Now, at dinner with French wine lovers, special occasions, family get-togethers.

LA FERME DU MONT

La Ferme Du Mont	Première Côte
WINERY	WINE NAME
Grenache/Mourvèdre/Syrah	2010
VARIETY	YEAR
Côtes du Rhône, France	$22
ORIGIN	PRICE
	CLOSURE

Winemaker Stéphane Vedeau has earned plenty of attention from critics for the wines he produces in France's southern Rhône Valley. A busy man, he also makes wines in Spain and consults with other wineries. His own label, La Ferme Du Mont, focuses on the wines of the Rhône, and he's striving to produce wines without the use of pesticides or artificial fertilizers. This Côtes du Rhône reveals a broad spectrum of aromas and flavours, running the gamut from tar, black licorice and plum sauce to leather and dried flowers. The flavours just last forever. A fun—and funky—wine worth checking out.

TRIVIA Powerful winds coming from the north, called "the mistral," have been known to damage vines in the southern part of the Rhône Valley.

PAIR WITH Lamb, wild game, burgers or cassoulet.

UNCORK Dinners with wine geeks and Francophile wine lovers, barbecues.

FIRST, THE RED WINES

MICHEL LYNCH

Michel Lynch	Bordeaux	
WINERY	WINE NAME	
Organic Merlot	2010	
VARIETY	YEAR	
Bordeaux, France	$16	
ORIGIN	PRICE	CLOSURE

Producer Jean-Michel Cazes—owner of the legendary Château Lynch-Bages—came up with the idea for this label as a way to pay homage to Michel Lynch, the former owner of the chateau and a winemaking pioneer who lived in the 1700s. It can be difficult to find a good Bordeaux in the under-$25 price range, but this organic entry is certainly worth a try. Expect fruits such as raspberry, plum, currant and cherry with a shot of nice oak spice and vanilla. The fruit is a tad restrained, in the Bordeaux style, but it has solid structure, and the tannins are very refined. It comes from Graves, on Bordeaux's Left Bank.

TRIVIA Merlot is the most-planted grape in Bordeaux. One of the world's most expensive wines—hello, Château Petrus—is primarily based on Merlot.

PAIR WITH Roast duck, herbed chicken, hamburgers, sausage, pasta with wild mushrooms.

UNCORK With wine geeks, on Earth Day or during Earth Hour, at special family dinners. Or put it away for a couple of years.

PARALLÈLE 45

Paul Jaboulet Aîné	Parallèle 45	
WINERY	WINE NAME	
Grenache/Syrah	2010	
VARIETY	YEAR	
Côtes du Rhône, France	$20	
ORIGIN	PRICE	CLOSURE

An earlier vintage of this wine was featured in the 2013 edition of *Uncorked!* One of the best-known names in France's Rhône Valley, Paul Jaboulet is the estate behind this red blend (60 percent Grenache, 40 percent Syrah), which gets its name from the 45th parallel, a circle of latitude that is 45 degrees north of the Earth's equator and runs just two kilometres (1.2 miles) from the winery's cellars.

While the Paul Jaboulet Aîné estate was started in the early 1800s, a family of champagne producers bought it in 2006; their daughter, Caroline Frey, is now the winemaker for the Paul Jaboulet Aîné wines, too. This  is a classic Côtes du Rhône, with flavours of plum, licorice, blackberry, vanilla and a bit of Twizzlers Nibs.

TRIVIA The 45th parallel also runs through other significant wine regions, including Oregon, Piedmont and southern Ontario. During the summer solstice, at this latitude, the sun is visible for 15 hours and 37 minutes; during the winter solstice, it's visible for 8 hours and 46 minutes.

PAIR WITH Sausages, burgers, lamb kebabs.

UNCORK Movie nights, game nights, family get-togethers.

FIRST, THE RED WINES

PLAN DE DIEU

Gabriel Meffre	Plan de Dieu "Saint-Mapalis"
WINERY	WINE NAME
Syrah/Grenache/Carignan	2010
VARIETY	YEAR
Côtes du Rhône Villages, France	$14
ORIGIN	PRICE

CLOSURE

"Plan de Dieu" literally means "the Plain of God," and is a reference to the land where the grapes are grown, one of the top villages in the Côtes du Rhône Villages appellation. Wine has been made at the Gabriel Meffre winery since 1936, and these days the team is also behind the perennially popular Fat Bastard wines. (You can find them in Canada, too.) As for this rich red blend, it features delicious notes of smoked meat, black licorice, blueberry and plum.

TRIVIA According to strict Côtes du Rhône Villages wine laws, at least 50 percent of a red blend must be made with Grenache grapes.

PAIR WITH Roast duck, grilled sausage, lamb roast, tagines, French cheese.

UNCORK With Francophiles, French folk and wine geeks.

SAINT COSME

Château de Saint Cosme	Saint Cosme
WINERY	WINE NAME
Syrah	2011
VARIETY	YEAR
Côtes du Rhône, France	$21
ORIGIN	PRICE	CLOSURE

If you want to talk wine history, check out Château de Saint Cosme. The estate in the southern Rhône Valley has been used for making wine since the year AD 109! By comparison, the stone chapel on the labels is a mere babe: it was built in 1109. These days, winemaker Louis Barruol makes some of France's best wines. This fruity, slightly jammy Côtes du Rhône is made completely from Syrah, and it's bursting with blueberry, blackberry, plum, strawberry, vanilla and black licorice.

TRIVIA The Château de Saint Cosme property has been in Louis Barruol's family since 1490, two years before Columbus discovered America.

PAIR WITH Roast duck, beef, lamb.

UNCORK Watching the History Channel, weeknight dinners, birthday parties, block parties.

SAINT COSME
2011
CÔTES-DU-RHÔNE

G.

Ktima Lantides Estate	G.
WINERY	WINE NAME
Agiorgitiko	2010
VARIETY	YEAR
Nemea, Greece	$25
ORIGIN	PRICE	CLOSURE

An earlier vintage of this wine appeared in the 2013 edition of *Uncorked!* Take a good look at this label. Guess, just guess, how some women like to order it. That's all we are saying on that subject.

Sure, the gold letter and big spot are attention getters, but the wine inside is what will make you come back for more. It's big, elegant and stylish, with notes of dried herbs, cherry, cranberry and vanilla. It, um, hits the spot. Winemaker Panos Lantides studied in Bordeaux before starting his own winery in Greece in 2000. It's a bit of a family affair these days; his son, Andreas, handles North American marketing. As for Panos, he makes wines from a variety of international grapes (Merlot, Cabernet Sauvignon, et cetera), as well as various Greek grapes, including Agiorgitiko (St. George), an indigenous Greek

variety that's used here. Greek isn't the world's easiest language, but try saying *Agiorgitiko* by pronouncing the letter "g" as a "y."

TRIVIA One of the world's most beloved saints, St. George was a Roman soldier who was martyred in AD 303. The grape named after him—Agiorgitiko—is one of Greece's most important indigenous grapes.

PAIR WITH Grilled lamb, prime rib, roasted Mediterranean-style vegetables. Or cellar it for a few years.

UNCORK With wine geeks, Christmas Eve, Easter, third dates, any time you feel like doing your bit to relieve the Greek debt crisis.

ARELE

Tommasi Viticoltori	Arele	
WINERY	WINE NAME	
Red blend (see below)	2010	
VARIETY	YEAR	
Valpolicella Classico, Veneto, Italy	$19	
ORIGIN	PRICE	CLOSURE

Tommasi celebrated its 100th birthday in 2012. Four generations after it was started, it's now led by six descendants of the original winery founders. (Giancarlo Tommasi is the winemaker.) The actual estate is located in the heart of the Valpolicella Classico wine region, and while the Tommasi team is justifiably famous for its Amarone (expensive, rich red Italian wines), this red blend—made from Corvina Veronese, Rondinella, Oseleta and Merlot grapes—is considerably more affordable. Yet, like Amarone, some of the grapes used in this blend were partially dried (*appassimento* means "to dry, or shrivel") to increase the intensity of the wine's flavours, which include raspberry, black cherry, licorice and vanilla.

TRIVIA The Veneto didn't officially become part of Italy until 1866; it is now the most-visited part of the country, with about 63 million tourists each year.

PAIR WITH Hard cheeses, rich stews, game or grilled meats.

UNCORK Now, with dear friends on cold winter nights, after a game of shinny, with a book by the fire.

FIRST, THE RED WINES

DANZANTE

Danzante	Chianti
WINERY	WINE NAME
Sangiovese	2010
VARIETY	YEAR
Chianti, Tuscany, Italy	$15
ORIGIN	PRICE	CLOSURE

Danzante was created out of a joint partnership between Marchesi de' Frescobaldi, an Italian company with a winemaking history spanning 700 years, and Napa Valley's Robert Mondavi Winery. Members of the Frescobaldi family—Italian royalty—are still actively involved in the wine industry and occasionally come to Canada to promote the wines.

Danzante, which means "dancing" in Italian, focuses on approachable, easy-going wines that represent different wine regions in Italy. To be called a Chianti, a wine must be made in the Chianti region of central Tuscany. This Chianti is made from 100

percent Sangiovese, and boasts aromas of violets, cherry, raspberry, vanilla and licorice.

TRIVIA King Henry VIII, of noted appetite and girth, was apparently a fan of the Frescobaldis' Tuscan wines.

PAIR WITH Pasta with meat sauce, mushroom dishes, steak, grilled sausages.

UNCORK Before a night of dancing, weekday dinners, block parties, watching *Dancing with the Stars*.

GELSO NERO

Podere 29	Gelso Nero	
WINERY	WINE NAME	
Nero di Troia	2011	
VARIETY	YEAR	
Puglia, Italy	$23	
ORIGIN	PRICE	CLOSURE

The name of this winery goes back to the First World War, when the Italian government numbered the land that was given to ex-soldiers after the war. "Podere" is Italian for a big old farmhouse and land, and *29* simply refers to the number that was given to the property by the government. Beyond the history, there's something very cool about this wine: it comes from a rare grape, Nero di Troia, one of the eldest indigenous grapes in Puglia, the "heel" of Italy's boot. You'll be charmed by its earthy, tart flavours of sour cherry, leather, blackberry, spice, tobacco and licorice.

TRIVIA St. Nicholas—yes, the bearded fellow we know best as ol' St. Nick—was born in Bari, Puglia's capital city. December 6—the anniversary of his death in AD 343—is still marked by children around the world as St. Nicholas Day. The saint's feast day—as it is also known—is also celebrated by followers of the Catholic Church.

PAIR WITH Spaghetti and meatballs, braised oxtail stew, steak, sausages.

UNCORK With Italophiles and real Italians, on St. Nicholas Day, Christmas Day, family gatherings, watching European soccer on the tube.

FIRST, THE RED WINES

PLANETA LA SEGRETA

Planeta	La Segreta	
WINERY	WINE NAME	
Red blend (see below)	2011	
VARIETY	YEAR	
Sicily, Italy	$20	
ORIGIN	PRICE	CLOSURE

An earlier vintage of this wine appeared in the 2013 edition of *Uncorked!* Perhaps Sicily's most famous and most exciting winery, Planeta was started in the 1980s by three siblings—all still actively involved. Their success has been phenomenal, and they now own vineyards across the island. While Planeta is best known for some of its pricier wines, wine lovers in search of a deal won't want to miss this entry-level (aka more affordable) red. This balanced and savoury blend of Nero d'Avola, Merlot, Syrah and Cabernet Franc

boasts red fruits such as redcurrant and sour cherry with black raspberry and notes of leather, toast and vanilla.

TRIVIA La Segreta is named after a forested area that surrounds the vineyards where the grapes are grown.

PAIR WITH Pastas with a Bolognese sauce, sausages, pizza, ratatouille.

UNCORK Friday night dinners, foreign film nights, *Planet of the Apes* marathons, while organizing your vinyl records.

PRIMITIVO FEUDI DI SAN GREGORIO

Feudi di San Gregorio	Primitivo di Manduria	
WINERY	WINE NAME	
Primitivo	2010	
VARIETY	YEAR	
Puglia, Italy	$18	
ORIGIN	PRICE	CLOSURE

Different vintages of this wine have appeared in all three editions of *Uncorked!* The Feudi di San Gregorio estate is located on some of the oldest wine-producing land in what is now Italy. Records show that wine grapes were grown there as far back as AD 590—the year considered to be the start of the Middle Ages. Feudi di San Gregorio was started in the mid-1980s in Campania, which wasn't particularly known for its wines outside of Italy. But the folks at Feudi di San Gregorio—who specialize in showcasing the

region's indigenous grapes—have done a lot to put it on the map for wine lovers. Manduria, by the way, is a city located just inside the high-heel part of the "boot" that forms the peninsula of Italy.

TRIVIA Primitivo is the 12th-most-common grape in Italy. Or so they say. It's also Italian for "Zinfandel."

PAIR WITH Italian sausages, meatball sandwiches, steak, short ribs.

UNCORK For NHL playoffs, dinner with Italophiles, dinner with wine geeks.

FIRST, THE RED WINES

ROCCA DELLE MACÌE

Rocca delle Macìe	Chianti Classico
WINERY	WINE NAME
Sangiovese/Merlot	2010
VARIETY	YEAR
Chianti Classico, Tuscany, Italy	$18
ORIGIN	PRICE

CLOSURE

This picture-perfect estate in the heart of the Chianti Classico wine region isn't just a winery; it's an agritourism operation, too, with beautiful little Tuscan homes-away-from-home for tourists to rent. You'll feel like you're ensconced in a Tuscan dream—and the wine is wonderful, too. Sangiovese is the official grape of the region and, according to Italian law, at least 80 percent of a Chianti Classico wine must be made from this dark-skinned grape. So, yes, this wine is made

from Sangiovese, with about 5 percent Merlot added into the mix. Expect a spicy, earthy, medium-bodied wine with notes of leather, sour cherry and plum; pair it with food to taste it at its best.

TRIVIA Ever watched a spaghetti western? Italo Zingarelli, the guy who started Rocca delle Macìe, once produced them. One of his most famous was *They Call Me Trinity*.

PAIR WITH Tomato-based pasta dishes, *bistecca alla fiorentina* (aka steak as they eat it in Tuscany), stews, game.

UNCORK Now, with wannabe actors, any time you wish you could run away to Italy and live *la dolce vita* every day.

TRESCONE

Lamborghini	Trescone	
WINERY	WINE NAME	
Merlot/Sangiovese/Ciliegiolo	2008	
VARIETY	YEAR	
Umbria, Italy	$25	
ORIGIN	PRICE	CLOSURE

Here's the wine for car lovers. This winery was started by Ferruccio Lamborghini, an Italian businessman who made a lot of money building tractors. But he's better known for the exotic sports car company he started in 1963. The story goes that Lamborghini wasn't totally satisfied with the Ferraris he'd been buying. When owner Enzo Ferrari rebuffed his criticisms, Lamborghini decided to make his own cars. The rest is history. Maybe that's why he started a winery, too—who knows?

What we do know is that this full-bodied blend includes Ciliegiolo, a red grape native to Umbria. Look for notes of vanilla, smoke, sour cherry, pepper, cloves and tobacco.

TRIVIA Trescone is a traditional dance performed in the region during the harvest.

PAIR WITH Spaghetti and meat sauce, grilled steaks.

UNCORK After detailing the car, while watching Formula One racing or the Barrett-Jackson auto auctions.

VILLALTA

Casa Girelli	Villalta Valpolicella Ripasso
WINERY	WINE NAME
Red blend	2010
VARIETY	YEAR
Valpolicella, Veneto, Italy	$19
ORIGIN	PRICE

CLOSURE

UNCORKED!

A passion for winemaking has been handed down, generation after generation, at this family-owned winery. It was started in the late 1800s in Trentino, Northern Italy, and is now apparently Italy's fourth-largest winery, with vineyards across the country. Sometimes called a super-Venetian, this wine is made in the Ripasso style, which means it's made with vino that has been "repassed" over a percentage of lightly dried grapes, similar to how Amarone (an intense and expensive

Italian red wine) is made. Expect this crowd-pleaser to have big jammy notes of blackberry, cherry and strawberry.

TRIVIA The history of partially drying grapes to make *appassimento* wines (a style that includes Ripasso and Amarone) in the region dates back to the time of the ancient Greeks, thousands of years ago.

PAIR WITH Stews, tagines, grilled red meats of all kinds.

UNCORK Now, on cold winter nights, with super-Canadians. Or cellar for a few years.

VILLA MEDORO

Villa Medoro	Montepulciano d'Abruzzo	
WINERY	WINE NAME	
Montepulciano	2009	
VARIETY	YEAR	
Abruzzo, Italy	$23	
ORIGIN	PRICE	CLOSURE

Located near the community of Medoro, just 13 kilometres (8 miles) from the Adriatic Sea on Italy's east coast, Villa Medoro has been producing wines since 1966. But the family-owned winery really started getting attention in 1997 when daughter Federica Morricone took over and put the focus on quality. This is a meaty, savoury wine with blackberry, plum, toast, vanilla, spice and cherry aromas and flavours. Incidentally, Montepulciano d'Abruzzo is one of Italy's most widely exported wines.

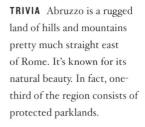

TRIVIA Abruzzo is a rugged land of hills and mountains pretty much straight east of Rome. It's known for its natural beauty. In fact, one-third of the region consists of protected parklands.

PAIR WITH Grilled beef, lamb or sausage, mushroom pizza.

UNCORK Neighbourhood barbecues, block parties, winter dinners.

FIRST, THE RED WINES

RABBIT RANCH

Rabbit Ranch		
WINERY		
Pinot Noir	2009	
VARIETY	YEAR	
Central Otago, New Zealand	$22	
ORIGIN	PRICE	CLOSURE

UNCORKED!

Pinot Noir is a finicky grape that requires a lot of TLC. That usually means you have to pay a lot for good quality. But not here. Central Otago is one of the buzz-worthy regions for Pinot Noir, and Rabbit Ranch delivers a great wine at a nice price. There are lots of secondary notes to this wine, which means extra complexity. The nose delivers cranberry, dried cherry, tea, spice, cedar and forest floor aromas. The palate is similar. With lively acidity and a long, lingering finish, this is a wine for careful contemplation. Drink it now.

TRIVIA The story goes that sheep and rabbits lived together at Rabbit Ranch until the rabbit population, as it's known to do, skyrocketed. Soon there was no room for the sheep. The owner gave up on sheep and planted vineyards instead.

PAIR WITH *Lapin à la cocotte* (a fancy French name for rabbit stew), mushroom risotto, duck confit.

UNCORK Thanksgiving, Easter (kidding!), first dates.

WHITEHAVEN

Whitehaven		
WINERY		

Pinot Noir	2011	
VARIETY	YEAR	

Marlborough, New Zealand	$25	
ORIGIN	PRICE	CLOSURE

An earlier vintage of this wine appeared in the 2013 edition of *Uncorked!* We always love stories like this one—the couple who started this winery fled high-powered careers in finance and marketing to pursue the bucolic winery life in New Zealand. (Translation— they probably worked even harder at the winery, but at least at the end of their day they could drink something delicious that they'd made.) Marlborough, perhaps New Zealand's most famous wine region, is especially renowned for its Sauvignon Blanc wines, but delicious Pinot Noir, such as this

one, is certainly worth checking out. Expect tons of cherry, tea, violet and cedar notes in a balanced package with a long finish.

TRIVIA New Zealand was the first country in the world to give women the right to vote, and it was the first country to introduce retirement pensions—just in case you needed more reasons to love the place after trying its outrageously good wines.

PAIR WITH Grilled salmon, duck with cherry sauce, roast chicken or roast turkey.

UNCORK Book club gatherings, holiday dinners, reunion parties.

CAVALO BRAVO

Parras Vinhos	Cavalo Bravo	
WINERY	WINE NAME	
Red blend (see below)	2010	
VARIETY	YEAR	
Tejo, Portugal	$15	
ORIGIN	PRICE	CLOSURE

The name of this wine, translated to English, literally means "brave horse," but you don't have to be brave to drink it; it's really very friendly and approachable. A blend of Trincadeira, Aragonez (another name for Tempranillo) and Castelão, it has savoury, earthy notes of cherry, coffee and cranberry. It's tasty.

TRIVIA Though this wine is under screw cap, Portugal supplies most of the corks used to seal many of the world's wines. The corks come from the bark of a specific oak tree. The removal of the bark doesn't harm the tree; instead, a new bark forms. That bark can be harvested again about a decade later.

PAIR WITH Barbecued ribs, pizza, tomato-based pasta dishes.

UNCORK Stampede gatherings, tailgate parties, watching football or World Cup soccer on TV.

PROVA

Monte da Ravasqueira	Prova
WINERY	WINE NAME
Red blend (see below)	2010
VARIETY	YEAR
Alentejano, Portugal	$13
ORIGIN	PRICE	CLOSURE

Although you may think only of port when you think of Portugal, the country is also renowned for its wonderful, rich, value-priced table wines, many proudly made from indigenous Portuguese grapes. This ruby-red wine is made with two such grapes—Aragonez and Trincadeira. Fruity, soft and ready to drink now, it is named after the Portuguese word for "proof," as in, here's proof the winemaking team knows what they're doing. Indeed, the family-owned winery is modelled after major Napa estates,  with considerable attention being put toward wine tourism. (There's a restaurant on-site, for instance.)

TRIVIA The winery is also home to a privately owned antique carriage museum, a nod to the fact the land was once used to raise Portugal's famous Lusitano horses.

PAIR WITH Tapas, pizza, barbecue, steak.

UNCORK Watching World Cup soccer games, casual gatherings with friends, with wine geeks.

VINZELO

Quinta de Ventozelo	Vinzelo
WINERY	WINE NAME
Red blend (see below)	2006
VARIETY	YEAR
Douro, Portugal	$18
ORIGIN	PRICE
		CLOSURE

Cistercian monks were the first people to cultivate grapes and make wine on the land that is now Quinta de Ventozelo. Long after the monks, the Ventozelo winemaking team made bulk port to sell to the region's myriad port houses. These days, however, they're creating some outstanding and very affordable dry table wines, including this friendly sipper. It's made from a slew of Portuguese grapes—Tinta Roriz, Touriga Franca, Tinta Barroca, Touriga Nacional—and it features flavours of mocha and cherry and a floral note, too.

TRIVIA Cistercian monks lead lives that revolve around manual labour, especially agriculture, hence the focus on grape-growing and cultivation. They are named after "Cistercium," the Latin name for the village of Citeaux in France.

PAIR WITH Barbecue, ribs, roast chicken, pizza.

UNCORK With good friends, wine geeks, casual Friday gatherings.

BOER & BRIT

Boer & Brit	The Field Marshal
WINERY	WINE NAME
Red blend (see below)	2010
VARIETY	YEAR
Western Cape, South Africa	$20
ORIGIN	PRICE

CLOSURE

What do you get when the great-great-grandsons of two of South Africa's most bitter rivals get together? Why, great wine, of course. Boer & Brit is headed by Stefan Gerber and Alex Milner. The pair met while studying winemaking and became fast friends. Their ancestors, though, were not so close. Gerber's great-great grandfather was Paul Kruger, one of the leaders of the Boer uprising against Britain. Milner is related to Field Marshall John French, a British military leader who fought the Boers. This medium-full-bodied, friendly red is a blend of Shiraz,

Mourvèdre, Tinta Amarela, Carignan and Grenache. It has aromas of licorice, cherry, blackberry and violet, with plenty of fruit and structure. Share it with an enemy, and you'll soon have a friend.

TRIVIA The Krugerrand, a gold coin with a value based on its actual gold content, not a preset price, is named after Paul Kruger. It also bears his picture.

PAIR WITH Grilled meats, roast beef, veal parmigiana.

UNCORK Dinner with the boss, weekend barbecues, recovering from battles at the office.

ANCIANO

Anciano	Gran Reserva 10 Years
WINERY	WINE NAME
Tempranillo	2002
VARIETY	YEAR
Valdepeñas, Spain	$15
ORIGIN	PRICE

CLOSURE

UNCORKED!

While we often see Spanish wines in our market, wines from the region of Valdepeñas —which means "valley of rocks"—are considerably more rare here; most are consumed within Spain itself.

Anciano, meaning "old" in Spanish, is certainly the right name for this wine, which was aged for a decade. But boy, is it holding up well. All that time in oak barrels has brought vanilla, toast, spice and leather to the forefront, but there's fruit, too: blackberry and black cherry. The finish is long with

a great balance between fruit, acid and tannin. Take a sip and travel back in time to 2002.

TRIVIA In 2002, the Euro currency started circulation, the Canadian dollar hit an all-time low of US 61.7 cents, and Canada's men's hockey team won its first Olympic gold medal in 50 years in Salt Lake City, Utah.

PAIR WITH Duck confit, squash soup, hearty stews.

UNCORK Family gatherings, retirement parties, anniversaries.

AYLES

Pago Aylés	A	
WINERY	WINE NAME	
Red blend (see below)	2011	
VARIETY	YEAR	
Cariñena, Spain	$20	
ORIGIN	PRICE	CLOSURE

This is a juicy wine from a special piece of property. It's classified as a "Pago" wine, which is a Spanish term for a wine from a unique and important vineyard—kind of like a Grand Cru vineyard in Burgundy. It's a rare classification, with just over 10 wineries in Spain earning such an honour. This blend of Merlot, Tempranillo, Garnacha (Grenache in France) and Cabernet Sauvignon is medium-full-bodied with currant and raspberry aromas and flavours. It has some tannic bite and a bit of spice.

TRIVIA Wines have been produced in this area of Spain since the mid-1100s.

PAIR WITH Lamb stew, *jamón ibérico* (Iberian ham), a juicy steak or by itself.

UNCORK When you want to impress your wine-geek friends, while watching Spanish soccer or Javier Bardem movies.

CAMPO VIEJO

Campo Viejo	Rioja Reserva	
WINERY	WINE NAME	
Red blend (see below)	2007	
VARIETY	YEAR	
Rioja, Spain	$23	
ORIGIN	PRICE	CLOSURE

For a time, when Roman soldiers were successful in battle, they were rewarded with land in an area of Spain known as Campus Veteranus ("Campo Viejo" comes from this name). Wine lovers will be rewarded with this complex blend of Tempranillo, Graciano and Mazuelo. A full-bodied wine, it delivers flavours of blackberry, black cherry, olive, plum and vanilla.

TRIVIA Native to the Rioja region of Spain, the Tempranillo grape got its name from *temprano,* which means "early" in Spanish. The grape ripens earlier than many other red grapes in the region.

PAIR WITH Lamb chops, chicken tagine, grilled chorizo.

UNCORK Fridays after work, special occasions, birthday parties.

CASTAÑO

Familia Castaño	Castaño	
WINERY	WINE NAME	
Monastrell	2011	
VARIETY	YEAR	
Yecla, Spain	$13	
ORIGIN	PRICE	CLOSURE

This family-owned winery has a few different vinos in the Alberta market, and every year one makes it into the latest edition of this book. This year, this one stands out because it's extra, extra good value. Made from vines averaging at least 30 years of age, this Monastrell (aka Mourvèdre) is full-bodied with lots of ripe tannins. (Get out the decanter.) But there's a lot more there than

just tannin. Watch for licorice, violet, black cherry, blackberry, earth and leather notes, too. As for the term "old vines," many winemakers believe that the older the vines for red wine grapes, the more intensely flavourful the grapes—and therefore the wines—will be.

TRIVIA "Castaño" means "chestnut tree."

PAIR WITH A juicy steak, roast duck, lamb burgers.

UNCORK When you want your guests to think you spent a lot more money than you actually did. Could be cellared for a few years.

FIRST, THE RED WINES

CASTILLO DE MONSÉRAN

Castillo de Monséran		
WINERY		
Garnacha	2010	
VARIETY	YEAR	
Cariñena, Spain	$11	
ORIGIN	PRICE	CLOSURE

A previous vintage of this wine was featured in the first edition of *Uncorked!* The Monséran winery produces only one kind of wine: Garnacha (known in France as Grenache), grown in an area of Spain that's been cultivating wine grapes since the days of the ancient Romans. Back then, the fermented grape juice was mixed with honey, but we don't recommend that these days. Rather,

just enjoy this value-priced vintage, with its flavours of blackcurrant, Twizzlers Nibs, licorice and pepper.

TRIVIA One of Spain's most famous artists, Francisco de Goya, was born in Cariñena; he influenced the work of myriad painters, including Édouard Manet, Pablo Picasso and Francis Bacon.

PAIR WITH Tomato-based pasta dishes, tapas. Or just enjoy by itself.

UNCORK With artists, bullfighters, World Cup soccer games, after you pay your taxes.

EL PETIT BONHOMME

Nathalie Bonhomme	El Petit Bonhomme	
WINERY	WINE NAME	
Monastrell/Garnacha/Syrah	2011	
VARIETY	YEAR	
Jumilla, Spain	$13	
ORIGIN	PRICE	CLOSURE

An earlier vintage of this wine appeared in the 2013 edition of *Uncorked!* Nathalie Bonhomme, formerly of Montreal, makes great wines—at outstanding prices—in Spain. She used the facilities of Bodegas Juan Gil, another outstanding winery, to create this beefy yet playful blend of Monastrell, Garnacha and Syrah. Behind a bit of a tannic mask, the flavours include rich blackberry,

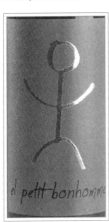

raspberry, leather, violet, vanilla, spice and plum. It's got just the right amount of sweet jamminess to pull it all together into a delicious package.

TRIVIA Nathalie Bonhomme worked in catering in South Africa before moving to Spain where she began exporting Spanish wine to Canada and other countries. Then she started making her own wines.

PAIR WITH Steaks, burgers and hard cheeses like manchego.

UNCORK Weekdays, weekends and holidays, family gatherings, barbecues, Saturday night hockey.

FIRST, THE RED WINES

ERGO

Bodegas Martín Códax	Ergo	
WINERY	WINE NAME	
Tempranillo/Garnacha	2009	
VARIETY	YEAR	
Rioja, Spain	$17	
ORIGIN	PRICE	CLOSURE

Named after a medieval singer from Galicia (in northwest Spain), Bodegas Martín Códax was established in 1986. That makes the winery a relatively new player on the Spanish wine scene when you think about the nation's long history with the grape. Although the winery itself is located near the western coast of Spain, Bodegas Martín Códax makes a very fine wine from Rioja in the country's

north-central region, too. Nicely balanced, this one has flavours of blackberry, plum, spice, toast, vanilla and even some hints of violet.

TRIVIA Ancient Phoenicians—from what we now call Lebanon—likely brought wine culture to Rioja.

PAIR WITH Hearty tapas bites, grilled pork ribs, beef on a bun.

UNCORK When you're trying to impress a wine snob, movie nights. Or put it in the cellar for a few years.

JUAN GIL

Bodegas Juan Gil	Juan Gil
WINERY	WINE NAME
Monastrell	2011
VARIETY	YEAR
Jumilla, Spain	$21
ORIGIN	PRICE

CLOSURE

If you like Châteauneuf-du-Pape, an expensive blend from France's Rhône Valley, you might like this wine, from one of Spain's best-known wine families. This full-bodied red is made from Monastrell, aka Mourvèdre, a grape often used in blends from the southern Rhône Valley. Expect a lot of lovely, soft tannins and ripe fruit: plum, blackberry and violet. The high alcohol content, 15 percent,

gives the perception of sweetness, but the wine is dry, and you really won't notice the alcohol level.

TRIVIA Three generations of this family-owned winery have shared the given name of Juan Gil.

PAIR WITH Paella, roast lamb, blue cheese.

UNCORK With Francophile wine lovers, dinner with the boss. Or lose a bottle or two in the cellar for a few years.

FIRST, THE RED WINES

LA VENDIMIA

Bodegas Palacios Remondo	La Vendimia	
WINERY	WINE NAME	
Tempranillo/Garnacha	2011	
VARIETY	YEAR	
Rioja, Spain	$21	
ORIGIN	PRICE	CLOSURE

Different vintages of this wine have appeared in all three editions of *Uncorked!* Born into a family that's been making wine for more than 350 years, Alvaro Palacios—one of five boys—spent his childhood playing in his parents' Rioja winery. Now an internationally famous winemaker, he studied in Bordeaux and then made his name with an expensive wine called L'Ermita.

La Vendimia is no second-class bargain, however. It's deep purple in colour with notes  of blackberry, earth, toast, vanilla and leather. It's a big wine that would improve with time in the cellar.

TRIVIA The Vendimia Grape Harvest Festival has been held in Jerez, Spain, for more than 500 years. "Vendimia" translates to "vintage." Other vendimia festivals are held throughout Spain and the world.

PAIR WITH Lamb ragout, cassoulet, pasta with meat sauce.

UNCORK Weekday dinners, birthday parties, afternoons by the fireplace.

MONTEREBRO

Bodegas Monterebro	Barrica
WINERY	WINE NAME
Monastrell	2010
VARIETY	YEAR
Jumilla, Spain	$20
ORIGIN	PRICE

CLOSURE

The name "Monterebro" is a combination of three Spanish words: *monte* (which means "mountain"), *terra* (the earth) and *ebro* (the River Ebro, which runs very near the winery). Monterebro is very, very modern, with a full winemaking team, and new equipment and ideas, but there's a strong nod to the past here, too. The winery's roots date back to the late 1800s, and quite a few of the vines are old, too, which many believe leads to richer-flavoured fruit. This full-bodied Monastrell, which is also called Mourvèdre or Mataró, depending on whom you're talking to, comes

from vines that are at least 60 years old. The wine has plenty of tannins, but underneath that layer, you'll find licorice, blackberry, cherry, spice and vanilla. There's about 15 percent Syrah in it, too, for an extra kick.

TRIVIA Monastrell—a red-skinned grape that typically makes high-tannin, high-alcohol wines—represents more than 85 percent of the vines planted in Jumilla.

PAIR WITH A juicy beef stew, spicy Mediterranean-style sausages, pizza, lasagna.

UNCORK With Shiraz fans (introduce them to something new), for movie nights and Sunday barbecues.

TRIDENTE

Bodegas Tritón	Tridente	
WINERY	WINE NAME	
Tempranillo	2009	
VARIETY	YEAR	
Castilla y León, Spain	$23	
ORIGIN	PRICE	CLOSURE

The Gil family is behind this winery, and for long-time fans of Spanish wine, that's a big deal. The Gils and their myriad winemaking projects—scattered across the country—are legendary for producing interesting wines of great depth and value. (Other labels include Juan Gil, Cellers Can Blau and Atalaya, to name just three.) This deep-ruby red—made from Tempranillo grapes—continues the trend. Look for notes of black cherry, leather, earth and tobacco, with a medium-plus finish and a lot of tannic backbone.

TRIVIA In ancient Greek mythology, Triton was the son of Poseidon. He was a messenger of the sea who could stop the waves with his conch-shell trumpet. He carried a trident, a three-pronged spear that looks a bit like a pitchfork.

PAIR WITH Lamb, duck, tuna steaks or burgers.

UNCORK Now, with legendary friends and wine geeks.

VERANO

Verano		
WINERY		
Shiraz	2011	
VARIETY	YEAR	
Valencia, Spain	$12	
ORIGIN	PRICE	CLOSURE

Although this wine comes from Spain and has a very Spanish name, it was actually created by two Canadian winemakers based in Niagara, Ontario. Heidi Montgomery works at Peller Estates, and Craig McDonald at Hillebrand Winery. The wine was made in Spain, but shipped in bulk wine tankers to Canada, where it was bottled. It's a Spanish wine, not a Cellared in Canada wine, because it contains no Canadian juice. Complicated? A little. The wine, however, is not. This super-

quaffable sipper features lots of big, juicy berry flavours, and it would be a great base for sangria.

TRIVIA "Verano" means "summer" in Spanish.

PAIR WITH Barbecue, roast chicken, grilled sausages.

UNCORK Patios, warm summer nights, camping trips, casual gatherings with friends.

FIRST, THE RED WINES

BALLARD LANE

Ballard Lane		
WINERY		

Cabernet Sauvignon	2010	
VARIETY	YEAR	

Paso Robles, California, US	$23	
ORIGIN	PRICE	CLOSURE

One of the most important wine families in California's Santa Barbara County is behind the Ballard Lane brand. The Miller family, who played a key role in the growth of the wine industry in the area by providing excellent fruit from their legendary Bien Nacido Vineyards, are involved in the Ballard Lane brand of value-based wines. The wine is made at one of the custom-crush facilities they own. Custom-crush operations are one-stop shops where small wineries can make

wine without having to invest in all the equipment. This Cabernet Sauvignon is worth investing in. It'll pay you back with flavours of plum, mocha, coffee, cassis, black raspberry, redcurrant and spice.

TRIVIA Paso Robles is located halfway between Los Angeles and San Francisco. Although it's famous for its wines and hot springs, the name literally means "the pass of the oaks."

PAIR WITH Anything big and meaty. Or just enjoy by itself.

UNCORK While watching Superman rescue Lois Lane, the desperate housewives of Wisteria Lane or any movie with Diane Lane.

CASTLE ROCK

Castle Rock		
WINERY		
Pinot Noir	2010	
VARIETY	YEAR	
Sonoma County, California, US	$18	
ORIGIN	PRICE	CLOSURE

Castle Rock is a winery without a winery. Rather than investing in expensive buildings and equipment, the team uses other people's winery facilities. They don't own vineyards, either. Instead, long-term leases are struck with grape growers. Everything is done to keep costs down so they can offer great wines at reasonable prices. This ruby-red Pinot Noir is a strong example; it offers flavours of black raspberry, black cherry, vanilla, allspice and smoke.

TRIVIA California First Nations legends refer to Sonoma as the "Valley of the Moon"; now, each fall, the Valley of the Moon Vintage Festival celebrates the area's many wineries.

PAIR WITH Cedar-planked salmon, pork, duck confit, veal, lamb souvlaki.

UNCORK Anniversaries, birthdays, Saturday night dinners.

CONUNDRUM

Conundrum		
WINERY		
Red blend	2010	
VARIETY	YEAR	
California, US	$25	
ORIGIN	PRICE	CLOSURE

The Wagner family entered the wine business in 1972 with Caymus Vineyards and eventually added a slew of brands, including Mer Soleil, Belle Glos and Conundrum. The Conundrum tale began 20 years ago with a white blend. Then, two years ago, they added this complementary red blend. And they are puzzlers. The family won't say what grapes are in either blend. It makes it kind of fun as you try to unlock the riddle. This sumptuous and soft red blend has floral/herbal notes plus aromas of smoke, blackcurrant, eucalyptus, vanilla and cedar. Grab a bottle and give it your best guess. This is a great choice for fans of white wine who are looking to give reds a try.

TRIVIA A conundrum is a type of riddle where the answer involves a pun. We'd make one up as an example, but we're not that sharp. Maybe we need more Conundrum.

PAIR WITH Hotdogs, smokies, hard cheeses or as an aperitif.

UNCORK While watching the Riddler on old *Batman* episodes, playing Trivial Pursuit, weekday unwinding, beach parties, campfire wiener roasts.

COPPOLA ROSSO & BIANCO

Francis Ford Coppola Winery	Rosso	
WINERY	WINE NAME	
Red blend (see below)	2011	
VARIETY	YEAR	
California, US	$15	
ORIGIN	PRICE	CLOSURE

Francis Ford Coppola is one of the few celebrities who have turned their attention to wine—and done it exceptionally well. The filmmaker and five-time Academy Award winner has a long string of major films to his credit, including *Apocalypse Now, The Godfather* trilogy, *Bram Stoker's Dracula, The Outsiders* and *Peggy Sue Got Married.*

But instead of focusing solely on Hollywood, he opted to pursue another great passion, too: winemaking. He started his winery in Napa Valley in the mid-1970s, and still spends time, attention and money doing things right—the best vineyards, the finest techniques. This wine is more affordable than many of his label's wines and offers juicy, crowd-pleasing notes of strawberry jam, cherries and mocha. And just in case you want to know the specifics, Rosso (Italian for "red") is a blend of Syrah, Cabernet Sauvignon, Zinfandel and Petite Sirah.

TRIVIA Coppola used his Napa estate as collateral when he needed money for filming *Apocalypse Now.* "This film is a $20-million disaster," he said at the time, according to *Wine Spectator.*

PAIR WITH Italian meatballs (the winemaking team's recommendation), pizza, pasta with tomato sauce, lasagna.

UNCORK Now, with good friends, for casual Friday night dinners, watching Coppola's classics.

DANCING BULL

Dancing Bull
....
WINERY

Zinfandel   2011
....
VARIETY   YEAR

California, US $14
....
ORIGIN   PRICE   CLOSURE

Take the bull by the horns and buy this wine.
We have no idea why this winery is called
Dancing Bull, but we do know that it's owned
by Gallo, one of the biggest wine companies
in the US. While the team at Dancing
Bull makes a range of wines, they focus on
Zinfandel, which does extremely well in parts
of California. This full-bodied Zinfandel
blend (it contains a wee bit of Petite Sirah
and Tempranillo) is big, brash and juicy, with
loads of cherry, raspberry and spice notes.

TRIVIA A bull is an
uncastrated male from the
Bos taurus (cattle) species.
When fully grown, they can
weigh up to about 1,000
kilograms (2,200 pounds),
and they are incapable of
seeing the colours red and
green. Or dancing, but don't
tell that to the winemaker.

PAIR WITH Burgers, pizza,
pasta with tomato sauce,
spare ribs.

UNCORK Bullfights, discos,
china shops.

DEEP SEA

Conway Family Wines	Deep Sea Red
WINERY	WINE NAME
Red blend (see below)	2008
VARIETY	YEAR
Central Coast, California, US	$24
ORIGIN	PRICE	CLOSURE

Talk about an appropriate name. This blend of Syrah, Petite Sirah, Lagrein, Merlot and Mourvèdre is as black and inky as the depths of the ocean. With 15 percent alcohol, it really coats the mouth, but there's so much ripe black fruit you almost don't notice the high octane level. The flavours of blackberry, plum, raspberry, cherry, vanilla and licorice linger forever in the mouth. This wine is produced by Conway Family Wines—Chris and Ann Conway and their five children. Their Deep Sea wines are made from grapes grown in cooler vineyard areas near the Pacific Ocean.

TRIVIA The Deep Sea tasting room is on the ocean, located on a wharf overlooking the sea in Santa Barbara, California. All seven members of the Conway family are certified scuba divers.

PAIR WITH Bison, steak, roast beef.

UNCORK When you're diving into a new adventure, parties with wine lovers, impressing first dates, convocation get-togethers.

EVOLUTION

Sokol Blosser	Evolution Red
WINERY	WINE NAME
Red blend (see below)	Non-vintage
VARIETY	YEAR
Oregon, US	$24
ORIGIN	PRICE	CLOSURE

A previous vintage of this wine appeared in the 2013 edition of *Uncorked!* Sokol Blosser is a family-owned winery that has been organic since it was created in 1971. While the team specializes in Pinot Noir, Evolution is a blend that changes slightly every year and, well, if there's Pinot Noir in it, no one's telling. Still, this light- to medium-bodied red—mostly Syrah, Sangiovese and Montepulciano—just might convert a white wine drinker into a red fan. Its cinnamon, cherry and raspberry flavours make it especially memorable.

TRIVIA In 1971, Tom Jones had a hit with "She's a Lady," Charles Manson was convicted of murder and locked up for life, Walt Disney World opened in Florida, and John Lennon released his song "Imagine."

PAIR WITH Roast chicken, gourmet flatbread pizza, duck, pasta, tagines, pasta and meat sauce.

UNCORK Earth Day, Earth Hour, Friday nights with long-time friends, any time you feel like starting an Evolution.

FIRST PRESS

First Press Wine Cellars	First Press
WINERY	WINE NAME
Cabernet Sauvignon	2010
VARIETY	YEAR
Napa Valley, California, US	$22
ORIGIN	PRICE

CLOSURE

First Press is one of the many wineries overseen by DFV Wines, a wine empire built by one of California's longest-serving wine families. Delicato Family Vineyards began in 1924 when Gasparé Indelicato planted his first vineyard in Napa Valley after immigrating from Sicily, Italy. Now two grandsons—Chris and Jay Indelicato—oversee a company with more than 10 different labels. First Press focuses on two wines: a Cabernet Sauvignon and a Chardonnay from Napa Valley. The Cab is an earthy, spicy wine with flavours of plum, blackberry, sour cherry, redcurrant, vanilla and leather.

TRIVIA The first wine press was likely the human foot, as prospective vintners walked on their grapes to squeeze the juice out. Some wineries in Portugal still use this method for their premium ports, though machines have been created to mimic the action of tramping on grapes.

PAIR WITH Herb-roasted chicken, grilled pork, wild mushrooms, stews, steak.

UNCORK Family Day, winter equinox, long weekends, dinner with the boss.

FLEUR

Fleur de California	Fleur
WINERY	WINE NAME
Pinot Noir	2010
VARIETY	YEAR
Central Coast, California, US	$25
ORIGIN	PRICE

CLOSURE

Francis and Kathy Mahoney were living in San Francisco when they heard the vineyard's call. They pulled up stakes, headed north toward Napa Valley and, in 1972, started building the first winery in the Carneros AVA (American Viticultural Area) since Prohibition. They started Fleur de California, with a focus on value wines, in 1987. There's certainly great value in this beautiful and compelling Pinot Noir. It's fresh and pure, with flavours of cherry, spice, forest floor, strawberry and vanilla.

TRIVIA "Carneros" means "ram" in Spanish. It's believed the area became known as Carneros because it was home to a lot of sheep and dairy farmers.

PAIR WITH The winemaker suggests portobello mushrooms with garlic, paté appetizers or smoked salmon.

UNCORK After a day of gardening, at garden parties, Sunday dinners, long weekends.

GHOST PINES

Louis M. Martini Winery	Ghost Pines Winemaker's Blend	
WINERY	WINE NAME	
Cabernet Sauvignon	2010	
VARIETY	YEAR	
Napa Valley and Sonoma County, California, US	$19	
ORIGIN	PRICE	CLOSURE

A previous vintage of this wine was in the first edition of *Uncorked!* Maybe you believe in ghosts. Maybe you don't. But after trying this wine, you will believe in Ghost Pines and, for that matter, affordable, good vino from California. If you want to impress friends with a red wine that punches above its weight, take this Ghost Pines with you. Full-bodied and supple with noticeable tannic structure, it features notes of red and black fruit, plus mocha flavours that linger nicely on the palate.

TRIVIA Depending on the type of tree they come from, pine cones can sometimes weigh close to five kilograms (that's about 10 pounds). Loggers used to call them "widow-makers" because one of these pine cones could kill a person if it landed on his head.

PAIR WITH Steak, burgers, pizza, ribs.

UNCORK Halloween parties with wine-loving friends, campfire ghost stories, casual Fridays.

FIRST, THE RED WINES

HESS SELECT

The Hess Collection	Hess Select
WINERY	WINE NAME

Cabernet Sauvignon	2009
VARIETY	YEAR

North Coast, California, US	$23	
ORIGIN	PRICE	CLOSURE

A wine from The Hess Collection—the family company behind this winery—has been in every edition of *Uncorked!* The family owns wineries around the globe, including South Africa, Australia, Argentina and, as you can see here, California. While this wine is mostly Cabernet Sauvignon (more than 80 percent), there are a few other grapes mixed in, too, including some Syrah and Merlot. This ripe, flavourful wine offers lots of structure, good tannins and vibrant acidity, as well as notes of blackberry, blueberry, vanilla, flowers and spice.

TRIVIA Donald Hess, who started the California estate, is one of the world's top art collectors. Many of the works he has gathered can be seen at The Hess Collection Winery in Napa Valley.

PAIR WITH Steak, roast beef, lamb, tagines.

UNCORK Now, with artists, art collectors and California wine fans.

J. LOHR

J. Lohr Vineyards and Wines	Seven Oaks	
WINERY	WINE NAME	
Cabernet Sauvignon	2010	
VARIETY	YEAR	
Paso Robles, California, US	$24	
ORIGIN	PRICE	CLOSURE

The son of a hard-working American farming family, Jerry Lohr holds a master's degree in civil engineering, and worked as a homebuilder before starting this winery in the early 1970s. It has grown considerably since those early days; now the team makes more than one million cases of wine each year. That's, oh, 12 million bottles if you count on 12 bottles in a case. This classic California Cabernet offers notes of blackcurrant, cherry, blackberry, mint and spice. Incidentally, the

J. Lohr website is exceptional, with wine and cheese pairing information, recipes and menu planning suggestions; go to jlohr.com if you want to check it out.

TRIVIA Lohr also created the world's first de-alcoholized wine, Ariel, by using a process called reverse osmosis.

PAIR WITH Steaks, ribs, roast beef, lamb, game.

UNCORK With farmers and homebuilders, homemakers and fans of big red wine. Or cellar for a few years.

LIBERTY SCHOOL

Hope Family Wines	Liberty School	
WINERY	WINE NAME	
Cabernet Sauvignon	2010	
VARIETY	YEAR	
Paso Robles, California, US	$19	
ORIGIN	PRICE	CLOSURE

UNCORKED!

Liberty School is one of five brands in the portfolio of Hope Family Wines. Hope Family is headed by Austin Hope, who was just in elementary school when his parents bought a ranch and moved to Paso Robles, California, in the 1970s. His parents planted vines on the property, and Hope was hooked. He learned the ropes in Napa Valley, then earned a winemaking degree and eventually bought the Liberty School winery. Liberty School shows what California can do so well—provide solid, reliable, fruit-forward wines year after

year. With blackberry, violet, mint, plum, vanilla and leather in a medium-full-bodied package, you won't want to skip this class.

TRIVIA Liberty School gets its name from the old schoolhouse in Rutherford, California, where the winery's founder (Charlie Wagner, who sold the winery to the Hopes) went to school.

PAIR WITH Roasted meats, including game.

UNCORK Relaxing after class, dinner with your parents, date night, graduation.

MATCHBOOK

Crew Wine Company	Matchbook	
WINERY	WINE NAME	
Syrah	2010	
VARIETY	YEAR	
Dunnigan Hills, California, US	$14	
ORIGIN	PRICE	CLOSURE

As a kid, winemaker John (JL) Giguiere was obsessed with fire—at one point, he even burned up one of his father's wheat fields. Fearing what was to come next, his father took him to the local jail, where the kid had to hang out for a while, learning what might come of him if he didn't back off from his pyromaniac proclivities. Good news for us, Giguiere eventually learned to put the matches down and took up winemaking. This juicy, medium- to full-bodied wine is beautifully complex, with notes of licorice, violets, red and black berries, spice and smoke—yes, seriously, but only a bit. There's about 10 percent Cabernet Sauvignon thrown into the Syrah, which comes from Dunnigan Hills in Yolo County, California.

TRIVIA Phillumeny is the hobby of collecting matchbooks, matchboxes, labels and the like; it comes from the words *phil* ("loving") and *lumen* ("light").

PAIR WITH Roast lamb, duck, bison, sausage.

UNCORK Backyard barbecues, nights at the cabin, around the campfire.

NOBLE TREE

UNCORKED!

Westside Winery	Noble Tree
WINERY	WINE NAME
Zinfandel	2008
VARIETY	YEAR
Sonoma County, California, US	$23
ORIGIN	PRICE

CLOSURE

If you like a lot of bang for your buck, you can't go wrong with this Zinfandel from California's Sonoma County. At 15.5 percent alcohol, there's certainly a lot of firepower in the bottle. But with a bounty of fruits, including blackberry, cherry, plum, blueberry and blackcurrant, and a higher acid level, you don't really notice the prodigious alcohol. It's just good, easy-drinking wine in a well-rounded package.

TRIVIA Westside Winery, which produces this wine, makes custom wines for anyone who wants their own private vino stash. You pick what kind of wine you want, how many cases, what the label should look like and—bam—a couple of months later you have a creative way to impress your friends.

PAIR WITH Barbecued ribs—beef or pork—plus burgers, beef stews or even grilled cheese.

UNCORK Christmas dinner, summer barbecues, garage sale unwinding, cold winter afternoons.

PB HEIN VINEYARDS

PB Hein Vineyards		
WINERY		
Syrah	2009	
VARIETY	YEAR	
Suisun Valley, California, US	$23	
ORIGIN	PRICE	CLOSURE

Paul Bernard Hein's family has been living in Napa Valley for five generations; in fact, his great-great-great-grandpa grew grapes on Napa's famous Mount Veeder way back when, before it was as famous among wine lovers as it is today. Hein started his career just making wines for fun, and then quickly realized people liked what he was doing. One thing led to another, and before long, he had a winery and he started winning awards. The rest, as the expression goes, is history.

The grapes for this gorgeous Syrah come from the Vernasco vineyard in the Suisun Valley, an American Viticultural Area (AVA) that borders Napa Valley and is about halfway between San Francisco and Sacramento.

Hein looks to Old World–winemaking techniques for inspiration, so expect a more restrained style of wine here: earthy, savoury, meaty, floral, ripe fruit notes, and a finish that goes on and on.

TRIVIA The label is a reproduction of *Black Moon Trailblazer*, a painting by Texas-based artist Michael Swearngin, who specializes in art inspired by American cowboy culture.

PAIR WITH Roast chicken, roast turkey, lamb dishes.

UNCORK With wine geeks, Sunday night dinners, Thanksgiving, Stampede parties.

FIRST, THE RED WINES

SEBASTIANI

Sebastiani Vineyards & Winery
....
WINERY

Cabernet Sauvignon   2009
....
VARIETY   YEAR

Sonoma County, California, US $24
....
ORIGIN   PRICE   CLOSURE

UNCORKED!

Samuele Sebastiani came to California from Tuscany, Italy, in 1895. A trained stonemason, he found work in Sonoma County quarrying cobblestones to be used in the streets of San Francisco. After years of scrimping and saving, he had enough money to buy land and start a winery in 1904. It continues to this day, making great, approachable wines like this soft, juicy sipper with plenty of fruit and a bit of sweetness. Look for notes of black licorice, blackberry, cassis, mint, vanilla and toast.

TRIVIA Sebastiani was the only winery in Sonoma County to make wines during Prohibition. The family kept the juice flowing by making sacramental wine and turning the winery into a cannery.

PAIR WITH Burgers, sausages, roast beef.

UNCORK Tailgate parties, graduation parties, movie nights, after detailing the car.

STEELHEAD RED

Steelhead Vineyards	Steelhead Red	
WINERY	WINE NAME	
Red blend (see below)	2009	
VARIETY	YEAR	
Sonoma County, California, US	$23	
ORIGIN	PRICE	CLOSURE

Good news for those of us who care about our environment—a portion of the proceeds from the sale of every bottle of Steelhead Red sold goes to Trout Unlimited to help conservation and restoration of steelhead trout and coho salmon populations in Northern California. And good news for wine lovers, too—this full-bodied blend is powerful and purple, with plummy, blackberry aromas, smooth tannins and a long finish. Although the makeup changes from vintage to vintage, the

2009 is 58 percent Zinfandel, 25 percent Cabernet Sauvignon and 17 percent Rhône grapes, including Syrah, Grenache and Mourvèdre.

TRIVIA Steelhead trout are the same species as rainbow trout; related to Pacific salmon, they are predators that eat smaller fish, fish eggs and insects. Yum.

PAIR WITH A big mess of ribs, lasagna, beef stew, hard aged cheddar. Or just enjoy by itself.

UNCORK Camping and fishing, NHL playoffs, football games, any time you need a crowd-pleasing reliable red.

THE WINERY

The Winery SF
....
WINERY

Petite Sirah   2008
....
VARIETY   YEAR

North Coast, California, US $25
....
ORIGIN   PRICE   CLOSURE

UNCORKED!

Did you know there's a winery located on a man-made island halfway between San Francisco and Oakland? We didn't—until now. The Winery SF operates on Treasure Island, which was constructed by the federal government in the mid-1930s. Measuring just under 2.6 square kilometres (one square mile), the island played host to the Golden Gate International Exhibition in 1939. This San Francisco neighbourhood is just off the Bay Bridge and not far from Alcatraz. While there are no vineyards here, the winery is open for tastings and tours, and it's proved plenty popular as a site for weddings.

This wine boasts powerful flavours of blackcurrant, cherry, leather, earth, vanilla, mint, eucalyptus and cedar in a full-bodied, high-tannin package. There's nothing petite about this Petite Sirah.

TRIVIA Treasure Island was indeed named after the classic adventure tale written by Robert Louis Stevenson, who lived in San Francisco for about a year in 1879.

PAIR WITH Beef tenderloin, roasted lamb, hard cheeses, barbecued ribs.

UNCORK While reading classic literature, Friday night get-togethers, movie nights.

TOAD HOLLOW

Toad Hollow Vineyards	Erik's the Red
WINERY	WINE NAME
Red blend (see below)	2009
VARIETY	YEAR
California, US	$24
ORIGIN	PRICE	CLOSURE

Toad Hollow was started by two good friends after they retired to California. They decided to start a winery because—don't we all?—they loved the good life. Since then, alas, those two friends have died, but the winery is still owned and operated by one of their wives ("Mrs. Toad," as she is referred to on the winery's website) and her business partner, Erik—hence, the wine's moniker, Erik's The Red. This kitchen-sink blend is made of red wine grapes sourced from across California. The blend changes from vintage to vintage, but the 2009 includes Merlot, Zinfandel, Cabernet Sauvignon, Souzão, Tannat, Syrah and Petite Sirah. The result is a deep, dark, stylish red, with lots of great cherry, raspberry and vanilla notes.

TRIVIA A group of toads is called a knot, and the bumps on a toad's back aren't warts but parotoid glands, which secrete a milky substance that helps deter predators.

PAIR WITH Prime rib, short ribs, gourmet homemade burgers.

UNCORK Barbecues, camping, any time someone says "bring a red" but doesn't tell you what's on the menu.

TRIM

Trim Wines	Trim	
WINERY	WINE NAME	
Cabernet Sauvignon	2010	
VARIETY	YEAR	
California, US	$19	
ORIGIN	PRICE	CLOSURE

The man behind this wine, Ray Signorello, is part of the Signorello family, one of the most famous names in the California wine business. But Ray holds dual US–Canadian citizenship. He grew up in Vancouver, went to the University of British Columbia, and now splits his time between California and Canada. He has several wine labels, including this one, and while the wine may be called "Trim", the flavours are far from thin. "The idea was to trim the costs and trim the fat, but still make

something that's real wine," he says. With that in mind, you'll find a lot of ripe fruit, including blackberry, black cherry, blackcurrant, vanilla, leather and plum. The flavours are vibrant and the tannins are fine-grained.

TRIVIA One of the world's most popular red grapes (only Merlot is more widely planted), Cabernet Sauvignon is a thick-skinned grape that is naturally high in tannin, the stuff that makes your mouth feel dry when you have a sip.

PAIR WITH Steaks, grilled lamb, roast beef.

UNCORK Movie nights, Sunday dinners with family, anniversaries, graduations.

AND
NOW,

THE
WHITE
WINES

CUMA

Michel Torino Estate	Cuma	
WINERY	WINE NAME	
Organic Torrontés	2012	
VARIETY	YEAR	
Cafayate Valley, Argentina	$14	
ORIGIN	PRICE	CLOSURE

Torrontés is the Rodney Dangerfield of grapes; it doesn't get much respect. But it should. Argentina produces some excellent wines from this homegrown aromatic grape that has a genetic link to Muscat of Alexandria (you can literally smell the connection). Enjoy the beautiful perfumed aromas of white blossom (some say freesia), lychee, apricot, nutmeg, stewed pear, spice and rose petal. The finish is long and flavourful.

TRIVIA The winery, which was started in 1892 by French brothers Salvador and David Michel, has produced organic wines since 2005.

PAIR WITH Asian dishes, chicken, curries. Serve chilled.

UNCORK Late lunches, when you're trying to impress a wine snob, first dates.

INTIS

Finca Las Moras	Intis	
WINERY	WINE NAME	
Sauvignon Blanc	2011	
VARIETY	YEAR	
San Juan, Argentina	$9	
ORIGIN	PRICE	CLOSURE

This Sauvignon Blanc comes from the Tulúm Valley, a sub-region of San Juan that is the same distance from the equator as Northern Egypt. And like Egypt, the Tulúm Valley is incredibly hot and dry, so dry that grape growing is only possible because of irrigation with water from the nearby river. While the area is best known for its rich red wines, some excellent, interesting whites are also made here, such as this one, from Sauvignon Blanc. There's a lot going on here: look for notes of gooseberry, slate, lemon and smoke.

TRIVIA The average grapevine needs about 635 to 890 millimetres (25 to 35 inches) of water each year to grow and create grapes.

PAIR WITH Sushi, seafood, smoked salmon. Serve chilled.

UNCORK Now, on takeout Tuesdays, casual Fridays, summer afternoons on the patio.

AND NOW, THE WHITE WINES

LA PUERTA

Valle de la Puerta	La Puerta
WINERY	WINE NAME
Torrontés	2011
VARIETY	YEAR
Famatina Valley, Argentina	$11
ORIGIN	PRICE · CLOSURE

If you like the musky, floral aromas of Gewürztraminer, try Torrontés. It shares many of the flavours and aromas you'll find in Gewürztraminer and Muscat. There are actually three different kinds of Torrontés grown in Argentina. Torrontés is the country's second-most-planted white grape, with 4,226 hectares (10,443 acres) under vine. For perspective, plantings of Malbec, the most-planted grape in Argentina, sat at 12,564

hectares (31,047 acres) at the end of 2011. This wine is bursting with flavours of lemon, apple, pear, melon, mineral, blossom and rose petal. "La Puerta" means "the door or gateway." Let this wine be your gateway to Torrontés.

TRIVIA Besides making top-notch wines, Valle de la Puerta also produces premium olive oils.

PAIR WITH Empanadas, fish, pork, chicken, Vietnamese food, or by itself. Serve chilled.

UNCORK Picnics, party starters, game nights, dinner with the parents.

PEWSEY VALE

Pewsey Vale
....
WINERY

Riesling   2011
....
VARIETY   YEAR

Eden Valley, Australia $18
....
ORIGIN   PRICE   CLOSURE

Pewsey Vale, near Adelaide in Australia's Eden Valley, was the first vineyard planted in the area. An English immigrant, Joseph Gilbert, planted grapes for wine in 1841. The vineyard, though, was abandoned until the 1960s when Geoffrey Angas Parsons, a lawyer wanting to get back to the land, bought it and replanted it. It's now a benchmark of the cool-climate Riesling that comes from the region. You'll find flavours and aromas of grapefruit, lime, mineral, chalk, lemon and green apple in this tart, dry wine.

TRIVIA The specific type of Riesling grape used at Pewsey Vale, called a clone in wine-geek speak, was first planted in the area in the 1800s. As well as growing grapes, Geoffrey Angas Parsons also raised champion shorthorn cattle.

PAIR WITH Oysters and other shellfish, Asian chicken dishes, sushi. Serve chilled.

UNCORK Mid-week dinners, buck-a-shuck oyster nights, afternoons at the cabin, after raking the leaves.

AND NOW, THE WHITE WINES

TAHBILK

Tahbilk
....
WINERY

Marsanne   2010
....
VARIETY   YEAR

Central Victoria, Australia $17
....
ORIGIN   PRICE   CLOSURE

An earlier vintage of this wine appeared in the 2013 edition of *Uncorked!* France's Rhône Valley may be the original home of Marsanne, but the Australian winery Tahbilk boasts some of the world's oldest Marsanne vines (some were planted in 1927). This medium-full-bodied wine oozes citrus and stone fruit flavours, including lemon, peach and apricot. They say it gets better with age, though in our houses it doesn't hang around long enough for us to find out.

TRIVIA Nagambie Lakes, the area this wine comes from, is located about 120 kilometres (75 miles) north of Melbourne. One of Australia's most famous characters, Ned Kelly, hailed from the region. Some refer to him as a hero. Others call him an outlaw. Either way, the man's short, violent life is still the stuff of books and movies, more than 100 years after his death.

PAIR WITH Sushi, halibut, fish and chips, sweet potato fries. Serve chilled.

UNCORK With gangsters, old-timers and history buffs.

YALUMBA

Yalumba	The Y Series	
WINERY	WINE NAME	
Viognier	2012	
VARIETY	YEAR	
South Australia, Australia	$17	
ORIGIN	PRICE	CLOSURE

Australia's oldest family-owned winery, Yalumba was founded in 1849 by Samuel Smith, who came to Australia from Britain, where he was involved in the brewing business. "Yalumba" means "all the land around" in the local Aboriginal language. This Viognier (*VEE-oh-nee-eh*) boasts lively peach, apricot, blossom, smoke, lemon and grapefruit aromas and flavours. If you like Chardonnay, you might like Viognier, which has a similar full-bodied texture.

TRIVIA The label says the wine is vegan and vegetarian friendly, meaning Yalumba doesn't use animal-based products when making wine, including eggs.

PAIR WITH Pork dishes, tagines, Asian salads. Serve chilled.

UNCORK While watching zany Australian comedies like *Strictly Ballroom* or *The Adventures of Priscilla, Queen of the Desert*.

AND NOW, THE WHITE WINES

CAVE SPRING

Cave Spring		
WINERY		

Riesling	2011	
VARIETY	YEAR	
Niagara Peninsula, Ontario, Canada	$22	
ORIGIN	PRICE	CLOSURE

UNCORKED!

Cave Spring is one of the driving forces of Ontario's wine industry. Leonard Pennachetti and his father, John, started the Cave Spring Vineyard in 1974, planting Riesling and Chardonnay in 1978. Then, with friend and winemaker Angelo Pavan, the Cave Spring winery was created in 1986 in the village of Jordan, Ontario. Through the years, a restaurant and two different inns have been added to the Cave Spring portfolio, bringing additional life to the cute community on the Beamsville Bench. But through it all, the wines have always remained the top focus.

This off-dry Riesling is a perfect example, delivering notes of peach, blossom, green apple and that chalky, wet-stone minerality you often find in Niagara Rieslings.

TRIVIA Cave Spring was one of the first Niagara wineries to offer a restaurant— On the Twenty—and accommodations—Inn on the Twenty and Jordan House.

PAIR WITH Citrus salads, roast chicken and curries. Serve chilled.

UNCORK Canada Day celebrations, Friday after-work get-togethers, bridal showers, birthday parties, family reunions.

CREEKSIDE ESTATE WINERY

Creekside Estate Winery
....
WINERY

Sauvignon Blanc **Niagara**	2011	
VARIETY	YEAR	

Niagara Peninsula, Ontario, Canada	$20	
ORIGIN	PRICE	CLOSURE

Located near the town of Jordan on the Niagara Peninsula, Creekside is a lovely, relaxing oasis of calm, with good food and, of course, wine. If you visit, you can sit on the winery's deck and sample a few vintages, or wander to the pond and check out the turtles, fish and frogs—always interesting to watch on a warm day. (The 16 Mile Creek runs alongside the property, too.) As for this wine,

you'll find it has lots of lively fresh lemon, lime peel, gooseberry and white peach notes.

TRIVIA Laura McCain, who started Creekside (but has since sold her interests), is part of Canada's famous McCain Foods family, the world's largest manufacturer of frozen potato products.

PAIR WITH Asian dishes, salads, asparagus. Serve chilled.

UNCORK Mid-week dinners, spring parties, after a day at the spa.

AND NOW, THE WHITE WINES

JACKSON-TRIGGS

Jackson-Triggs Okanagan Estate	Reserve	
WINERY	WINE NAME	
Chardonnay	2011	
VARIETY	YEAR	
Okanagan Valley, BC, Canada	$16	
ORIGIN	PRICE	CLOSURE

Started in 1993, Jackson-Triggs gets its name from Allan Jackson and Donald Triggs, who founded the winery in Ontario's Niagara region in 1993. This wine, however, comes from the winery's second estate, across the country in BC's Okanagan Valley. As for the wine, it features a good shot of citrus, green apple and tropical fruit. With just enough oak to round things out, it's a great wine to keep in the fridge to pour for unexpected guests.

TRIVIA Derek Kontkanen makes the white wines for Jackson-Triggs in the Okanagan Valley. When he's not making wine, he can often be found on his bike. He rides every year in a *gran fondo* ("long distance" in Italian) bike race in the Okanagan Valley.

PAIR WITH Whitefish with a citrus or cream sauce, warm Mediterranean-style roast vegetable salad. Serve chilled.

UNCORK Summer beach parties, watching sunsets, preferably in the Okanagan Valley.

L50

Gray Monk Estate Winery	L50	
WINERY	WINE NAME	
White blend (see below)	2011	
VARIETY	YEAR	
Okanagan Valley, BC, Canada	$17	
ORIGIN	PRICE	CLOSURE

The name of this winery comes from the Austrian and Hungarian translation for Pinot Gris, *Grauar Mönch,* which literally translates to "gray monk." In 2012, the Heiss family—which owns the winery—celebrated 40 years of growing grapes and 30 years of making wine. No one is confessing what the grapes are in this white, but if we had to guess, well, we'd say it has a bit of everything—maybe a little Chard, a little Pinot Gris, some Riesling and probably Gewürztraminer. But we're  just guessing, so you can guess, too. What we do know is that this wine—pretty and aromatic, with rose, lychee, lemon and spice notes—is a crowd-pleaser, and the sexy new label is, too. And if you like the white, look for the Latitude 50 red as well.

TRIVIA Latitude 50 degrees north is more or less where the Okanagan Valley (and Vancouver and Regina, too) fall on the globe.

PAIR WITH Asian takeout, salad, roast chicken, scallops. Serve chilled.

UNCORK Thanksgiving, Christmas, family gatherings, hot summer nights.

SANDHILL

Sandhill	King Family Vineyard	
WINERY	WINE NAME	
Pinot Gris	2010	
VARIETY	YEAR	
Okanagan Valley, BC, Canada	$19	
ORIGIN	PRICE	CLOSURE

UNCORKED!

Winemaker Howard Soon, who grew up in Vancouver, started his career making beer but eventually turned to wine and, since 1997, has been making outstanding wines at Sandhill in Kelowna. He especially focuses on single-vineyard wines—wines made from one particular plot of land. This Pinot Gris, for example, is from the King Family Vineyard north of Penticton. It offers honeysuckle, mineral, pear, spice and lemon flavours. The finish is fresh and leaves you wanting more.

TRIVIA The land where these grapes were grown has been farmed by the King family since the 1930s.

PAIR WITH Creamy pasta, white fish, salads. Serve chilled.

UNCORK After finishing the yard work, picnics at the beach, Canada Day celebrations, late afternoons on the patio, evenings at the lake.

SEE YA LATER RANCH

See Ya Later Ranch	Unleashed	
WINERY	WINE NAME	

Riesling	2011	
VARIETY	YEAR	

Okanagan Valley, BC, Canada	$22	
ORIGIN	PRICE	CLOSURE

If you've ever been to See Ya Later Ranch, you'll know the winery has a dog theme going on, with several wines named after the pooches of the late pioneering landowner Major Hugh Fraser. (There are dogs on the labels, too.) This wine is called Unleashed, appropriate since the palate is rather rowdy: full of zesty citrus flavours such as lime, grapefruit and lemon, plus tart green apple. It's dry and lively, and it goes so well with food.

TRIVIA Love dogs? Look for the "Winery Dogs of BC" calendar. Published every year, it features pooches from across the province. For information, go to polyglotpublishing.com or ask at your favourite BC winery.

PAIR WITH Creamy pasta, oysters. Serve chilled.

UNCORK While putting your feet up after taking the dogs for a walk or while watching the Westminster dog show on TV.

AND NOW, THE WHITE WINES

SUMAC RIDGE

Sumac Ridge Estate Winery	Cellar Selection
WINERY	WINE NAME
Pinot Grigio	2011
VARIETY	YEAR
Okanagan Valley, BC, Canada	$15
ORIGIN	PRICE CLOSURE

One of the oldest wineries in BC's Okanagan Valley, Sumac Ridge opened its doors in 1981 on land that was previously a golf course. Started by a fellow named Harry McWatters, it is now owned by Vincor, a subsidiary of Constellation, one of the world's largest wine companies. But forget about corporations for a minute and focus on this refreshing Pinot Grigio: it's full of bright lemon, apple, pear and lime zest notes, with just a bit of sweetness and orange blossom on the nose.

TRIVIA A sumac is a small tree, typically found in temperate areas of North America. Dried sumac wood will turn fluorescent under black light.

PAIR WITH Shrimp, white fish. Serve chilled.

UNCORK Sunday brunches, patio parties, after a day on the golf links.

VINELAND

Vineland Estates Winery	Unoaked Chardonnay	
WINERY	WINE NAME	
Chardonnay	2011	
VARIETY	YEAR	
Niagara Peninsula, Ontario, Canada	$19	
ORIGIN	PRICE	CLOSURE

Celebrating its 30th harvest in 2013, Vineland Estates is one of the most consistent wineries on Ontario's Niagara Peninsula, producing fresh, juicy wines year after year. The property has a top-notch restaurant with a beautiful view, a market store selling artisan products and a stone carriage house that can be rented for weddings and other events. In fact, this unoaked Chardonnay would be ideal for a wedding reception. Without that

oak influence, the focus is on vibrant fruit flavours such as grapefruit, lemon, green apple, pineapple and apricot. It has a tart zing to it and a long, balanced finish.

TRIVIA Vineland Estates offers wines in kegs, a storage method that is gaining momentum in Canada as by-the-glass purchases become more popular.

PAIR WITH Oysters and other shellfish, summer salads, trout and white fish. Serve chilled.

UNCORK Fish fries, anniversary dinners, spring feasts, watching the sunset.

AND NOW, THE WHITE WINES

WHITE KNUCKLE

Monster Vineyards	White Knuckle	
WINERY	WINE NAME	
White blend (see below)	Non-vintage	
VARIETY	YEAR	
Okanagan Valley, BC, Canada	$22	
ORIGIN	PRICE	CLOSURE

Monster Vineyards is a fun spin-off from Poplar Grove, one of the Okanagan's most prestigious wineries. While the term "white knuckle" means to be tense, afraid, apprehensive, you won't be any of those things when you taste this delicious beast of a blend. (It's Sauvignon Blanc, Gewürztraminer, Viognier and Riesling, if you care.)

TRIVIA Ogopogo is a monster that's reported to live in Okanagan Lake near the winery; the name means "lake demon" in the Salish First Nations language, and sightings go back to the 19th century.

PAIR WITH Scallops, prawns, lobster, roast chicken, goat cheese and fennel flatbread, grilled salmon, Asian takeout. Serve chilled.

UNCORK Now, with or without monsters, on patios, any time you need a reliable white but no one has told you what is on the menu.

CHÂTEAU L'OISELINIÈRE DE LA RAMÉE

Chereau Carré	Château l'Oiselinière de la Ramée	
WINERY	WINE NAME	
Melon de Bourgogne	2011	
VARIETY	YEAR	
Loire Valley, France	$20	
ORIGIN	PRICE	CLOSURE

The white wines of Muscadet, located in the Loire Valley near the Atlantic Ocean, are touted as the perfect match for shellfish, particularly oysters on the half-shell. You'll know why with just one taste. The flavour is a bit like the liquor, or water, you find in an oyster shell—steely, minerally and salty. Green apple and lime round out the flavours of this

light-bodied, high-acid wine. Château l'Oiselinière de la Ramée is the vineyard this wine came from. As for the Chéreau family, they have been making wine in this region since the 1400s.

TRIVIA The term *sur lie* also appears on the label. That means the wine was aged for a time with the dead yeast cells left after fermentation, like in champagne. The fancy name for dead yeast cells is "lees," or *lies* in French. The dead stuff may sound grim, but leaving the wine on the lees keeps it fresh while also adding more body and flavour.

PAIR WITH Oysters and shellfish, sushi. Serve chilled.

UNCORK Beach campfires, after a day of whale-watching (might have to leave Alberta for that one).

PETIT CHABLIS

Domaine Gérard Tremblay	Petit Chablis	
WINERY	WINE NAME	
Chardonnay	2011	
VARIETY	YEAR	
Burgundy, France	$22	
ORIGIN	PRICE	CLOSURE

Gérard Tremblay is carrying on a family tradition that goes back five generations. He crafts precise Chardonnays in the northern Burgundy commune of Chablis, which is known for fresh wines with vibrant acidity. This unoaked Petit Chablis is a perfect example of the region's style, with steely, almost smoky, oyster-shell aromas and tart green apple, pear, lemon and mineral flavours on the palate.

TRIVIA Although it's located pretty much in the middle of France, much of the soil around Chablis is made of fossilized oyster shells. This soil is thought to be the reason some wines from the area have an oyster-shell aroma and flavour, what the French call *gout de terroir*, or "taste of the earth."

PAIR WITH Oysters on the half-shell, assorted seafood, citrus salads, roast chicken or turkey. Serve chilled.

UNCORK Family holiday dinners, Saturday afternoons.

VOUVRAY

Domaine de Vaufuget	Vouvray
WINERY	WINE NAME
Chenin Blanc	2011
VARIETY	YEAR
Loire Valley, France	$23
ORIGIN	PRICE

CLOSURE

An earlier vintage of this wine appeared in the first edition of *Uncorked!* One of the world's most versatile white grapes, Chenin Blanc is used to make amazing dry wines, sweet wines and sparkling wines. Because of their high acidity, wines made from Chenin Blanc often improve for years in the bottle. It has been tested by time: the grape has a history in France's Loire Valley that goes back to AD 845.

Part of the Loire, Vouvray is particularly well known for making great Chenin Blanc. Pop the cork on this one from Domaine de

Vaufuget, and you'll find aromas and flavours of quince, apple, pear, lime peel, spice, lychee and honey. It's a bit sweet, but the high acid level keeps everything in balance.

TRIVIA Chenin Blanc is also known in France as Pineau de Loire and Pineau de Anjou. It's the most-planted grape variety in South Africa, where it's often called Steen.

PAIR WITH Seafood, stir-fries, cheese fondues, Indian and Mexican food with a bit of heat. Serve chilled.

UNCORK Family gatherings, bridal showers, book club meetings, garden parties.

DEINHARD

Deinhard	Green Label	
WINERY	WINE NAME	

Riesling	2010	
VARIETY	YEAR	

Mosel, Germany	$12	
ORIGIN	PRICE	CLOSURE

Deinhard's roots in winemaking run deep: the winery was founded in 1794 in Koblenz, an ancient city in Mosel, one of Germany's most important wine regions. The green colour on this label is designed to help wine neophytes identify it as being fruity and fresh. And that is exactly what you'll find: a soft and fresh Riesling, with green apple, lime peel, melon, petrol and peach flavours and aromas.

TRIVIA "Deinhard" means "strong warrior" in German, and was originally a first name, then became best known as a last name . . . and, of course, a wine.

PAIR WITH Pork chops, ham, Chinese or Thai takeout, mild curries, fruit salads. Serve chilled.

UNCORK At patio parties, casual Fridays, after hiking or spring housecleaning.

GRUEN

Gruen		
WINERY		
Riesling	2011	
VARIETY	YEAR	
Rheingau, Germany	$16	
ORIGIN	PRICE	CLOSURE

A different vintage of this wine appeared in a previous edition of *Uncorked!* In German, "Gruen" means "green." It's an apt word to describe this winery, which bills itself as climate-neutral. What does that mean? According the winery, everything—bottles, grapes, its production—must be handled in a way that leaves no harmful effect on the environment. While the wine might not be labelled organic, at least it's helping to reduce greenhouse

gases—something to consider, seeing that wineries ship their creations all over the world. When you pull this bottle out of the fridge, you'll find lovely flavours of white peach, lemon, lime peel, lychee and stone, with a medium-sweet, high-acid finish.

TRIVIA The Rheingau is one of 13 official wine regions in Germany. About 80 percent of the wine made in the region comes from Riesling.

PAIR WITH Spicy cuisine, sushi, white fish dishes, Indian takeout, Thai green curries. Or just enjoy it by itself. Serve chilled.

UNCORK After packing the camper, birthday parties, Friday night dinners, mid-week takeout.

AND NOW, THE WHITE WINES

SCHLOSS REINHARTSHAUSEN

Schloss Reinhartshausen	Classic
WINERY	WINE NAME
Riesling	2011
VARIETY	YEAR
Rheingau, Germany	$20
ORIGIN	PRICE

CLOSURE

The "Classic" designation found on this label means the wine hits several standards that are too confusing to go into (German labels can be particularly confusing). Mostly, it just means the wine is dry or off-dry (which means it's ever-so-slightly sweet). This classic Riesling comes from the Rheingau, a warm-ish region near Frankfurt, and it boasts aromas of lemon, blossom, pear, mineral and peach with a hint of diesel. A beautiful finish and lots of acidity mean this could stand up to all kinds of foods.

TRIVIA The word *schloss* is often found on German wine labels, and literally means "castle or palace."

PAIR WITH Asian dishes, fresh spring salads, turkey. Serve chilled.

UNCORK Dinner with friends, Thanksgiving, Christmas. It will cellar for a few years, too.

ST. URBANS-HOF

St. Urbans-Hof
WINERY

Riesling   2011
VARIETY   YEAR

Mosel, Germany $17
ORIGIN   PRICE   CLOSURE

Based in the Mosel Valley, St. Urbans-Hof is one of Germany's top Riesling producers. And it has a strong connection to Canada. Second-generation winemaker Hermann Weis brought Riesling vines to Ontario's Niagara Peninsula, planting a large vineyard in the 1970s. Called the St. Urban vineyard, the grapes are now tended by Vineland Estates Winery. This off-dry wine from the Mosel brings flavours of ripe lemon, apricot, blossom, lime peel and mineral.

TRIVIA The winery is named after the patron saint of German winemakers—St. Urban. "Hof," which means "estate" in German, was added to complete the title.

PAIR WITH Thai and Indian dishes, ham, white fish, salads with vinaigrette dressings, desserts or as an aperitif. Serve chilled.

UNCORK Hot summer days, with takeout food, first day of spring.

AND NOW, THE WHITE WINES

ROBOLA

Gentilini Winery and Vineyards	Robola of Cephalonia	
WINERY	WINE NAME	
Robola	2011	
VARIETY	YEAR	
Kefalonia, Greece	$25	
ORIGIN	PRICE	CLOSURE

A beautiful island where the movie *Captain Corelli's Mandolin* was set, Kefalonia is home to several fascinating indigenous grape varieties. Robola, many experts believe, likely found its way to Greece via traders who brought it from the Venetian islands. This example—made by British winemaker Mike Jones who now makes his home on Kefalonia—is crisp and dry, with flinty, lemon and floral notes.

The Gentilini winery was started in the 1970s, and while this Robola isn't organic, the family has been making a strong push toward organic wine production. Maybe next vintage? We'll see.

TRIVIA One of the Gentilini family's ancestors opened one of the first wineries in England. Yes, you read that correctly. Gerassimo Cambitzi opened Isleworth Wineries in 1929, just outside of London.

PAIR WITH Calamari, shellfish, sablefish, salmon. Serve chilled.

UNCORK With wine geeks, on hot summer days, while watching *Captain Corelli's Mandolin*.

MASIANCO

Masi	Masianco	
WINERY	WINE NAME	
Pinot Grigio/Verduzzo	2011	
VARIETY	YEAR	
Veneto, Italy	$14	
ORIGIN	PRICE	CLOSURE

The folks at Masi call this wine a super-Venetian, alluding to the non-traditional Bordeaux blends from Tuscany that became known as super-Tuscans. (Except this one is a white wine and it comes from the Veneto. Confusing? We agree.) Predominantly Pinot Grigio, Masianco also contains a bit of Verduzzo, a white wine grape mostly grown

in northeast Italy. The result is a fresh, zippy blend, with flavours of pear, green apple, orange, vanilla and a bit of pineapple.

TRIVIA The first written record of the Verduzzo grape dates back to June 6, 1409, when it was made into a wine served at a banquet in honour of Pope Gregory XII. Interestingly, this Gregory was the last pope to resign for 600 years, until Pope Benedict in February 2013.

PAIR WITH Grilled shrimp, scallops, salmon or fresh trout. Serve chilled.

UNCORK Bocce games, drinks at the 19th hole, book club gatherings.

AND NOW, THE WHITE WINES

MEZZACORONA

Mezzacorona
....
WINERY

Pinot Grigio   2011
....
VARIETY   YEAR

Trentino-Alto Adige, Italy $16
....
ORIGIN   PRICE   CLOSURE

Using grapes from 1,500 growers, Mezzacorona operates out of an über-modern winery that even boasts a concert auditorium. Despite the size of the high-tech operation where it's made, this Pinot Grigio is crafted with considerable attention to detail and features plenty of characteristic minerality from the hillside vineyards that run from Lake Garda to the Dolomite foothills. Besides that mineral tang, green apple, pear, spice

and orange blossom flavours can also be found.

TRIVIA The axe-shaped Lake Garda is Italy's largest lake. Opera singer Maria Callas had a villa on the lake where she could relax after her time on stage, and American poet Ezra Pound convinced his friend, fellow writer James Joyce, to join him at Lake Garda, writing that "the location is well worth the journey." Yes, they were all wine drinkers.

PAIR WITH Light fish dishes, salads, fried chicken, or by itself as an aperitif. Serve chilled.

UNCORK Summer evenings, mid-week relaxing, listening to opera and reading.

TIEFENBRUNNER

Tiefenbrunner		
WINERY		
Pinot Grigio	2011	
VARIETY	YEAR	
Trentino-Alto Adige, Italy	$19	
ORIGIN	PRICE	CLOSURE

Located in northeastern Italy, near the border with Austria, this estate has been in the Tiefenbrunner family since the 1600s. These days Herbert Tiefenbrunner and his son Christof head up operations, making more than 700,000 bottles per year. This Pinot Grigio has notes of pear, lemon, light apple, blossom and a touch of spice. And the finish—the taste that's left in your mouth after you swallow the wine—goes on and on.

TRIVIA Before the invasion of the Romans, the region of Trentino had been settled by the Celts, and in fact, the province of Trentino is named after Trent, the Celtic god of water.

PAIR WITH Butter scones, cucumber sandwiches, charcuterie. Serve chilled.

UNCORK Sun-kissed summer brunches, solstice parties, Sunday dinners.

AND NOW, THE WHITE WINES

TREBBIANO D'ABRUZZO

Jasci & Marchesani	Trebbiano D'Abruzzo	
WINERY	WINE NAME	
Organic Trebbiano	2011	
VARIETY	YEAR	
Abruzzo, Italy	$18	
ORIGIN	PRICE	CLOSURE

UNCORKED!

Sebastiano Jasci decided in 1978 to put his family winery's vineyards on an organic path, meaning no artificial fertilizers or herbicides could be used. You can't argue with the results. This Trebbiano is particularly intriguing. Imagine combining sweet blossoms, caramel and baked pears with brown sugar and an herb, maybe anise, and you'll be close to the aroma and flavour found in this delicious wine. Better yet, don't imagine it—go out and buy a bottle and make your own judgment.

TRIVIA Trebbiano is one of the world's most-planted wine grapes. In addition to growing throughout much of Italy, it's also found in France (where it's called Ugni Blanc), Portugal (where it's called Talia or Ugni Blanc), and Bulgaria, Russia, Greece and South America.

PAIR WITH Fruit salads, grilled chicken with a sticky Asian ginger sauce, sweet and sour pork. Serve chilled.

UNCORK Drinks with wine lovers, Friday night gatherings, after a night at the opera.

ASTROLABE

Astrolabe	Province
WINERY	WINE NAME
Sauvignon Blanc	2011
VARIETY	YEAR
Marlborough, New Zealand	$21
ORIGIN	PRICE	CLOSURE

A darling of the wine-geek crowd, Astrolabe is a small, independent winery named after a boat that sailed around the coast in the early 1800s. While the team makes a range of wines, including Riesling and Pinot Noirs, they focus on Sauvignon Blanc. This one is your textbook New Zealand style, loaded with juicy,

pungent, tropical fruit flavours. First comes the passion fruit, followed by stewed lemon, grass and then green pepper and spice. The finish just goes on and on.

TRIVIA Astrolabe isn't just a winery. It's also a sort of navigational tool used in ancient times.

PAIR WITH Roast chicken or turkey, asparagus, warm goat cheese dishes. Serve chilled.

UNCORK With wine geeks, or graphic designers who will love the stylish label.

MATUA VALLEY

Matua Valley		
WINERY		

Sauvignon Blanc	2012	
VARIETY	YEAR	

Hawke's Bay, New Zealand	$19	
ORIGIN	PRICE	CLOSURE

In New Zealand's native Maori language, "Matua" refers to the head of the family. It's an apt title since Matua Valley Wines, started in 1974 by brothers Ross and Bill Spence, was the first New Zealand winery to produce Sauvignon Blanc. We all know how that's gone. New Zealand now makes some of the world's top Sauvignon Blancs. This is a classic example, with zippy acidity, great balance and intense flavours of passion fruit, grass, lemon, grapefruit, smoke, gooseberry and blackcurrant leaf.

TRIVIA In 1974, the sitcom *Happy Days* hit TV. That same year Peter Benchley released the novel *Jaws*, about a killer great white shark. Director Steven Spielberg turned the novel into the first summer blockbuster movie in 1975, while *Happy Days* would "jump the shark" two years later.

PAIR WITH Niçoise salad, goat's cheese, citrus salads, ceviches, fish tacos. Serve chilled.

UNCORK Long summer weekends, family get-togethers, unexpected guests, rugby matches.

STONELEIGH

Stoneleigh Vineyards	Stoneleigh	
WINERY	WINE NAME	
Sauvignon Blanc	2012	
VARIETY	YEAR	
Marlborough, New Zealand	$16	
ORIGIN	PRICE	CLOSURE

Stoneleigh Vineyards gets its name from its "sunstones," the large stones found throughout the land. Once part of an ancient riverbed, they now absorb and reflect heat to help Stoneleigh's vines ripen their grapes. This wine isn't as pungent as some New Zealand Sauvignon Blancs, but you will find lots of that tropical fruit that fans expect, plus notes of grass, lemon, lime, passion fruit, gooseberry, blackcurrant leaf and bell pepper. We expect you to find them all, of course.

TRIVIA Marlborough is on New Zealand's South Island, the larger of the country's two main islands. In Maori, the country's indigenous language, it is sometimes called *Te Wai Pounamu,* a reference to the fact that the island is a source of greenstone, also known as jade.

PAIR WITH Salads, fried zucchini with garlic, asparagus, roast chicken. Serve chilled.

UNCORK On sunny days on the patio, with unexpected visitors, or after Saturday chores.

VILLA MARIA

Villa Maria Estate	Private Bin	
WINERY	WINE NAME	
Sauvignon Blanc	2012	
VARIETY	YEAR	
Marlborough, New Zealand	$17	
ORIGIN	PRICE	CLOSURE

Following his Croatian parents' wishes, Sir George Fistonich apprenticed as a carpenter before following his true passion: winemaking. In 2011, he celebrated 50 years as the founder, owner and CEO of Villa Maria, leading this family-owned winery to international acclaim. This crisp Sauvignon Blanc is one of the wines that made Villa Maria famous; it's crisp and clean, with zesty lemon and herbal notes.

TRIVIA Sir George Fistonich is the first New Zealander to ever be knighted for his contributions to his country's wine industry. The event earned him the honour of using the title "Sir" before his name. However, he cannot pass the honour on to his heirs, nor can he sell it.

PAIR WITH Fresh oysters, scallops, mussels, asparagus or salad. Serve chilled.

UNCORK Now, with time-tested friends, Croatians and knights.

THE WOLFTRAP

Boekenhoutskloof	The Wolftrap	
WINERY	WINE NAME	

White blend (see below)	2011	
VARIETY	YEAR	

Western Cape, South Africa	$13	
ORIGIN	PRICE	CLOSURE

The Wolftrap wines from Boekenhoutskloof (pronounced *BOOK-en-hoots-kloof*—say that three times fast) have been catching a lot of attention for being among South Africa's most consistent. The red blend is delicious. It was featured in the first two editions of *Uncorked!* But so is this medium-full-bodied white blend, which is built on Viognier and rounded out with Chenin Blanc and Grenache Blanc.

Look for aromas and flavours of peach, flower blossoms, grapefruit, lemon, flint and smoke, with a nice finish and a slightly oily texture.

TRIVIA Boekenhoutskloof began operations in 1776, the same year the United States was established. The winery is named after Boekenhout, a beech tree found in the area. Apparently it's very popular with furniture makers.

PAIR WITH Pasta salad, pad Thai, Indian pakoras. Serve chilled.

UNCORK With Red Riding Hood's grandma, late lunches, early dinners.

AND NOW, THE WHITE WINES

BOTANI

Jorge Ordóñez & Co.	Botani
WINERY	WINE NAME
Botani	2011
VARIETY	YEAR
Sierras de Málaga, Spain	$21
ORIGIN	PRICE	CLOSURE

UNCORKED!

Many popular wines made from the Muscat grape are vinified sweet, and lately there's been an explosion of them on the market. But this example from Spanish producer Jorge Ordóñez shows all the aromatic glory of this ancient grape. Look for aromas and flavours of melon, blossom, honey, herb, spice, lemon and green apple. And it's dry-off-dry, meaning you can drink another glass (or, for that matter, half the bottle) without getting a

sugar rush. But don't ask us. We aren't doctors. We just like to drink good wine.

TRIVIA Muscat of Alexandria is believed by grape experts (there is such a thing) to be one of the oldest genetically unmodified grapes in the world. It's so old, Cleopatra is believed to have enjoyed wine made from Muscat of Alexandria grapes, around 30 BC. There's no word if Mark Antony was also a fan.

PAIR WITH Asian dishes, roast chicken or turkey, desserts like crème brûlée, or as an aperitif. Serve chilled.

UNCORK Sunday brunches, turkey days, watching epics like *Spartacus, Ben-Hur* or *Cleopatra.*

VIÑA ESMERALDA

Torres	Viña Esmeralda
WINERY	WINE NAME
White blend (see below)	2011
VARIETY	YEAR
Catalunya, Spain	$14
ORIGIN	PRICE · CLOSURE

The Torres family has been making wine in Spain for more than 300 years, and while many of those wines are legendary, sometimes you just want something that's easy to drink. Easy to enjoy. Something you don't have to sit and ponder; you can just appreciate it from the very first sip. Here's your wine—a zippy, dry blend of Muscat of Alexandria (85 percent) and Gewürztraminer (15 percent). You'll find aromas of fresh flowers and green

grapes, and, on the palate, rose, banana and pineapple notes. As for the name "Esmeralda," it refers to the brilliant colour of the Mediterranean Sea.

TRIVIA Spain has more than 1.17 million hectares (2.9 million acres) planted with grapevines, more than any other country.

PAIR WITH Salads, Asian takeout or mussels. Serve chilled.

UNCORK Now, on hot summer afternoons, on the patio or at the beach.

AND NOW, THE WHITE WINES

BEAR FLAG

Bear Flag	Soft White Wine Blend
WINERY	WINE NAME
White blend (see below)	Non-vintage
VARIETY	YEAR
California, US	$14
ORIGIN	PRICE	CLOSURE

The state flag of California is known as the Bear Flag, thanks to the fierce grizzly in the middle of it. The illustrators who created the flag modelled the bear on a real bruin with a long story. It was 1889, and newspaper magnate William Randolph Hearst wanted to bring a live grizzly bear to San Francisco. Hearst sent one of his "cub" reporters (pardon the pun) to get him a bear. The reporter, who had no hunting experience, was eventually able to trap one a few months later. He brought it to San Francisco, and the bear, named Monarch, was put on display before being moved to the zoo. The Bear Flag was

based on Monarch. It's a wild story, and the wine's pretty wild, too—an offbeat and flavour-packed blend of Muscat of Alexandria, Symphony, Sauvignon Blanc, Chardonnay and French Colombard grapes, from the folks at E. and J. Gallo. It's very approachable, with floral, lemon and lime notes.

TRIVIA Eduarto Bertone is the artist behind the unforgettable Bear Flag labels. There's a different one for each of the four wines.

PAIR WITH Chicken souvlaki, Asian takeout, grilled chicken. Or just enjoy by itself. Serve chilled.

UNCORK Now, with good buddies, bargain hunting.

CHATEAU ST. JEAN

Chateau St.	Sonoma County Chardonnay	
WINERY	WINE NAME	
Chardonnay	2011	
VARIETY	YEAR	
Sonoma County, California, US	$17	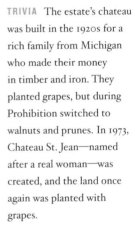
ORIGIN	PRICE	CLOSURE

An earlier vintage of this wine was in the 2013 edition of *Uncorked!* California Chardonnay sometimes gets knocked by know-it-all wine drinkers who think they don't like the Chardonnay grape, which pretty much once defined white wine in North America. But really, served slightly chilled, Chardonnay is incredibly food friendly and enjoyable. Year after year, Chateau St. Jean makes a reliable California Chardonnay at a very good price. Expect fresh notes of pear, lemon and pineapple, with a nice balance of fruit and oak. As for the name, "Jean" is pronounced like blue jeans and the "St." stands for saint. You don't need a French accent, unless you want to pronounce "château" correctly.

TRIVIA The estate's chateau was built in the 1920s for a rich family from Michigan who made their money in timber and iron. They planted grapes, but during Prohibition switched to walnuts and prunes. In 1973, Chateau St. Jean—named after a real woman—was created, and the land once again was planted with grapes.

PAIR WITH Grilled fish, beer can chicken, roast turkey, lobster with butter, fettuccini alfredo, souvlaki, creamy soups. Serve chilled.

UNCORK Family gatherings, first dates, dinner with the boss, Thanksgiving, Christmas.

AND NOW, THE WHITE WINES

HAYES RANCH

Hayes Ranch	Best Foot Forward	
WINERY	WINE NAME	
Chardonnay	2010	
VARIETY	YEAR	
California, US	$15	
ORIGIN	PRICE	CLOSURE

There are three Hayes Ranch wines—a Chardonnay, Cabernet Sauvignon and Merlot—and each has western gear (either a saddle, a cowboy boot, or a horseshoe) on its label. The name alludes to the Hayes family who owned a ranch near San Jose, California. The family found riches mining in Wisconsin and—at a time when newspapers made lots of money—they owned the *San Jose Mercury* and *Herald* newspapers. They also built a 41,000-square-foot mansion, with more than 200 rooms plus lodging for 40 ranch hands, on the ranch. Perhaps not surprisingly,

it is now used as a hotel. This rich, buttery California Chardonnay seems worthy of mansion life, with loads of ripe fruits, including apple, lemon and peach, as well as vanilla and smoky notes.

TRIVIA The widowed Mary Hayes-Chynoweth, who built the mansion with her two sons and their families, was a spiritualist who heard voices, one of which told her where her sons should start mining. The tip from the otherworld proved correct and they struck it rich.

PAIR WITH Fried chicken, baked ham, grilled pork. Serve chilled.

UNCORK Stampede parties, séances, Sunday dinners, Friday movie nights, unexpected guests from here or the hereafter.

KUNDE

Kunde Family Estate	Magnolia Lane
WINERY	WINE NAME
Sauvignon Blanc	2011
VARIETY	YEAR
Sonoma Valley, California, US	$22
ORIGIN	PRICE

CLOSURE

The Kunde family entered the wine business in 1904 in California's Sonoma Valley. Louis Kunde, a German immigrant, bought a vineyard that had been planted with vine cuttings from Bordeaux's renowned Châteaux Margaux and Lafite Rothschild. Now in their fifth generation of wine production, the Kundes grow their grapes on a 750-hectare (1,850-acre) estate. This California Sauvignon Blanc offers lovely fruit without being too pungent. Look for notes of lemon, gooseberry, passion fruit and green apple, plus zippy acidity and a lingering finish.

TRIVIA Kunde Family Estate was the 202nd winery to be registered and bonded in California. As of 2012, there were 3,754 wineries in California, according to the Wine Institute.

PAIR WITH The Kunde team recommends Ahi tuna skewers, lemon and shrimp risotto cakes, oysters on the half-shell, and an herbed omelette with goat cheese. Serve chilled.

UNCORK California wine parties, while sorting your vinyl record albums, fish fries.

AND NOW, THE WHITE WINES

MORNING FOG

Wente Vineyards	Morning Fog
WINERY	WINE NAME
Chardonnay	2011
VARIETY	YEAR
Livermore Valley, California, US	$15
ORIGIN	PRICE	CLOSURE

The Wentes could be considered America's first family of Chardonnay. Their winery, which celebrated its 130th anniversary in 2013, was the first in the US to produce a wine labelled as Chardonnay. In fact, a specific type of Chardonnay grape—the Wente Clone—is named after the family, and wineries across California use it. Grown from estate grapes that are cooled by the morning fog that wafts inland from the Pacific Ocean, this Chardonnay boasts flavours of apple, pear, lemon, vanilla, blossom and toast.

TRIVIA The Wente Vineyards have an 18-hole golf course designed by former golf champion Greg Norman, who's also in the wine business—but not with the Wentes.

PAIR WITH Creamy pasta, roast turkey, grilled chicken. Serve chilled.

UNCORK Weekday dinners, major anniversaries, block parties, potlucks, on the 19th hole.

RA! RA!
ROSÉ!
(PINK
DRINKS)

ARBOIS

Domaine Rolet Père & Fils	Arbois Aquarelle
WINERY	WINE NAME
Poulsard	2012
VARIETY	YEAR
Jura, France	$20
ORIGIN	PRICE	CLOSURE

UNCORKED!

Perched between Burgundy, France, and Switzerland, Jura is a bit off the beaten track, but it is also where some rather interesting wines are made. Domaine Rolet is a true family estate, with four members of the clan handling the winemaking and marketing at the winery that was started by their father, Désiré Rolet, in the 1940s. Made from the Poulsard grape, this bone-dry rosé from the Eastern French region of Jura offers flavours of green apple, lemon, grapefruit and currant.

TRIVIA Although Poulsard is a red grape (the experts call it a black grape), it's often used to make white wines in the Jura region. Its thin skin, similar to Pinot Noir, makes it easier to squeeze the juice out of the grapes without getting much colour.

PAIR WITH Salmon burgers, sausage, pasta with a rosé or tomato-based sauce, pizza. Serve chilled.

UNCORK Hot summer days, long weekends, block party barbecues, weekday dinners.

CLOS DU SOLEIL

Clos du Soleil	Rosé	
WINERY	WINE NAME	
Cabernet Sauvignon	2012	
VARIETY	YEAR	
British Columbia, Canada	$22	
ORIGIN	PRICE	CLOSURE

Former Navy commander Spencer Massie and partners fell in love with BC's Similkameen Valley in 2005 and decided to start a winery. They brought winemaker Ann Sperling, Massie's high-school classmate, on board in 2008. Sperling, who also makes wines for her own Okanagan label and for Southbrook Vineyards in Niagara, Ontario, has crafted a lovely, juicy rosé filled with spice, pear, cherry, violet and strawberry. This off-dry, medium-pink wine has a long finish and tons of flavour.

TRIVIA If you like this wine, I mean really like it, you can get it by the keg. Clos du Soleil offers several of its wines in kegs, a format gaining traction with restaurants that want more serving options.

PAIR WITH Thai dishes, curries, pizzas, desserts or as an aperitif. Serve chilled.

UNCORK Summer campfire sessions, Friday night unwinding, Sunday suppers.

RA! RA! ROSÉ! (PINK DRINKS)

DOMAINE DE NIZAS

Domaine de Nizas	Rosé
WINERY	WINE NAME
Syrah/Grenache/Mourvèdre	2011
VARIETY	YEAR
Languedoc, France	$20
ORIGIN	PRICE

CLOSURE

UNCORKED!

Domaine de Nizas was started in 1988 by John Goelet, an American with ties to French wine trader Daniel Guestier of Barton & Guestier fame. Goelet has built his own wine empire, with wineries in Australia (Taltarni, Clover Hill and Lalla Gully), Napa Valley (Clos du Val) and France's Languedoc (Nizas). Made from Grenache, Syrah and Mourvèdre, this pale salmon–coloured wine reveals wisps of dried rose petals, strawberry, cherry, apple and lemon pith.

TRIVIA The lovely label for this wine is based on two 18th-century sculptures by French artist Étienne-Maurice Falconet.

PAIR WITH Asian dishes, desserts, cucumber sandwiches. Serve chilled.

UNCORK While listening to angelic arias on the stereo, mid-week dinners, book club gatherings, Sunday brunches.

GALIL

Galil Mountain	Rosé	
WINERY	WINE NAME	
Red blend (see below)	2011	
VARIETY	YEAR	
Upper Galilee, Israel	$14	
ORIGIN	PRICE	CLOSURE

Galil Mountain is located on the Upper Galilee mountain range, a ridge of mountains on the Israeli border, looking toward Lebanon. Vines have been grown here for 2,000 years, so there's some history. The grapes used to deliver this refreshing dry rosé include Sangiovese, Barbera, Pinot Noir and Syrah. The combination creates a salmon-coloured wine with flavours of strawberry, raspberry, McIntosh apple, pear and light cherry. And as a bonus for anyone who's

Jewish, this wine is also kosher and kosher for Passover.

TRIVIA There are more than 150 wineries in Israel, which measures in at about 20,000 square kilometres (7,700 square miles). The size of Canada? About 10 million square kilometres (3.9 million square miles).

PAIR WITH White fish dishes, creamy pastas, desserts, brunches or as an aperitif. Serve chilled.

UNCORK Jewish holidays and celebrations, Saturday nights, block parties, Sunday brunches.

RA! RA! ROSÉ! (PINK DRINKS)

MARQUÉS DE CÁCERES

Marqués de Cáceres	Rosé	
WINERY	WINE NAME	
Tempranillo/Garnacha	2011	
VARIETY	YEAR	
Rioja, Spain	$15	
ORIGIN	PRICE	CLOSURE

A previous vintage of this wine was in the first edition of *Uncorked!* Marqués de Cáceres was started in the 1960s when Enrique Fornier, a Spaniard who owned properties in Bordeaux at the time, and French enologist Émile Peynaud decided to start making wine in Spain's Rioja region. Preferring a style more focused on fruit than oak, they paved the way for a different style of wine in Rioja. You certainly can't get much fresher than this dry rosé with notes of green apple, pear, peach, lemon, spice, cherry and a bit of orange rind.

TRIVIA The cellars of Marqués de Cáceres hold 10 million bottles. That would be a lot of trips to the recycling depot.

PAIR WITH Paella, Mediterranean vegetables, charcuterie, pasta, hotdogs. Serve chilled.

UNCORK Now, on a patio in the sun, any time you wish you could take a hot European holiday but can't afford it.

MISSION HILL

Mission Hill Family Estate	Rosé
WINERY	WINE NAME
Red blend (see below)	2012
VARIETY	YEAR
Okanagan Valley, BC, Canada	$15
ORIGIN	PRICE	CLOSURE

Year after year, from its lofty perch overtop the valley, Mission Hill manages to be one of the most consistent players in the Okanagan, no matter what the weather has been like. This wine, made predominantly from Merlot with some Pinot Noir and Cabernet Sauvignon, is perfect for sunny summer days. One sniff and you'll be transported to an Okanagan orchard, with aromas of strawberry, green apple, pear and raspberry enveloping you. A pleasant, fruity finish with a beam of acidity and just a touch of sweetness makes this a great patio sipper.

TRIVIA Anthony von Mandl, the owner of Mission Hill, also created Mike's Hard Lemonade, another refreshing summer drink.

PAIR WITH Citrus salads, grilled fish, poultry, Asian dishes with a bit of spice in them. Serve chilled.

UNCORK Outdoor weddings, bridal showers, Friday nights with friends, at the 19th hole.

RA! RA! ROSÉ! (PINK DRINKS)

ROSÉ DE TARGÉ

Château de Targé	Cabernet de Saumur
WINERY	WINE NAME
Cabernet Franc	2011
VARIETY	YEAR
Loire Valley, France	$25
ORIGIN	PRICE	CLOSURE

UNCORKED!

The Loire Valley is home to many of France's most historic castles and estates. Take a river cruise and you'll be awed by some of the structures. Château de Targé has its own lengthy history. It was purchased in 1655 by the personal secretary of Louis XIV and has remained in the family since. A modern winery was built in 1976. Made from Cabernet Franc, this off-dry wine is a pale salmon colour with flavours of cherry, strawberry, apple and lemon pith.

TRIVIA You can get a taste of being a Loire château owner by staying at the gîte—a vacation rental—on-site at the property.

PAIR WITH Tabbouleh, fruit pies, salads, or on its own. Serve chilled.

UNCORK With strawberries and cream and a new episode of *Downton Abbey,* afternoon tea (just substitute the rosé for the tea).

SIBLING RIVALRY

Henry of Pelham	Sibling Rivalry 11 Pink	
WINERY	WINE NAME	
Cabernet/Gamay/Syrah	2011	
VARIETY	YEAR	
Niagara Peninsula Ontario, Canada	$18	
ORIGIN	PRICE	CLOSURE

The three brothers behind Henry of Pelham—Paul, Matthew and Daniel Speck—all had other plans when they finished high school. Paul was going to be a lawyer, Matthew saw a future as a mechanical engineer while Daniel was thinking about a career in medicine. Instead they were all seduced by the wine world and joined the family winery.

Henry of Pelham was also among the first Ontario wineries to embrace European grape varieties when, in 1984, they pulled up most of their hybrids—grapes like Concord and Niagara—and replaced them with the

likes of Chardonnay and Riesling. This rosé, made from Cabernet, Gamay and Syrah, delivers zesty cherry, cranberry, raspberry, stone and blackcurrant flavours.

TRIVIA The Specks' great-great-great-grandfather Nicholas Smith farmed on the winery's land in 1794. His youngest son built the building that is now the winery. His name? Henry. And the winery's address? Pelham Road.

PAIR WITH Salmon, mac and cheese, citrus salads, pizza. Serve chilled.

UNCORK Unwinding at your golf course's 19th hole, Thanksgiving dinner, patio lunches.

RA! RA! ROSÉ! (PINK DRINKS)

SPY VALLEY

Spy Valley Wine	Rosé	
WINERY	WINE NAME	
Pinot Noir	2012	
VARIETY	YEAR	
Marlborough, New Zealand	$23	
ORIGIN	PRICE	CLOSURE

Here's a beautiful wine bursting with berries and roses. Made solely from Pinot Noir, this perfectly balanced wine from Marlborough is fresh, lively and deserving of a spot in your refrigerator.

The name "Spy Valley" comes from the fact that the winery is located near a real spy base—aka a "satellite communications monitoring base," according to the winery's website—in Marlborough's Wairau Valley.

TRIVIA The folks at Spy Valley follow all sorts of eco-friendly practices (minimal sprays, mulching). As part of those practices, they recycle their glass on-site, crushing it into dust that is then "mixed with mulch and distributed below the grapevines to enhance light reflection into the vines" (according to their website).

PAIR WITH Berries and ice cream, grilled salmon, charcuterie, sushi. Serve chilled.

UNCORK First day of spring, hot summer nights, weekend brunches, after hikes.

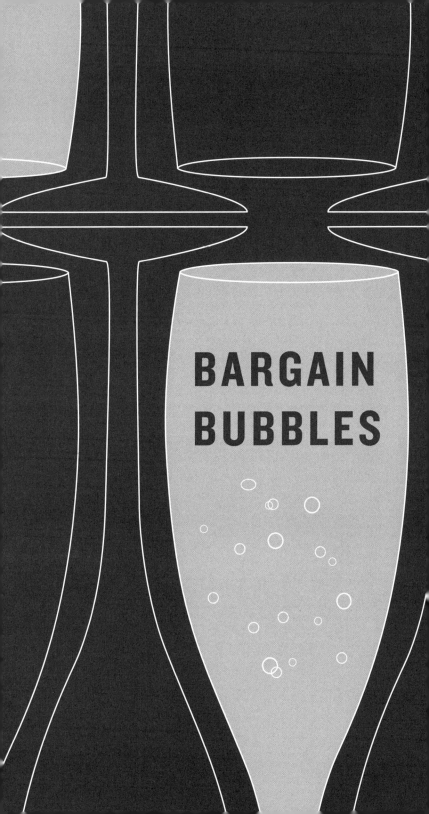

BARGAIN BUBBLES

ADAMI

Adriano Adami	Garbèl Brut	
WINERY	WINE NAME	
Prosecco	Non-vintage	
TYPE	YEAR	
Treviso, Veneto, Italy	$23	
ORIGIN	PRICE	CLOSURE

This wine appeared in the 2013 edition of *Uncorked!* By international law, Prosecco can only be made from Glera grapes, in Italy's Veneto region. This Prosecco comes from the Adami winemaking family near the city of Treviso, just northwest of Venice. They've been growing grapes and making Prosecco on this land since 1920, and by 1933, they were already winning awards for their fine bubbles. This sparkling treat features a fancy silk label and very enjoyable notes of lemon, pear and McIntosh apple.

TRIVIA "Garbèl" refers to a "crisp, dry, slightly tart wine" in one of the region's ancient local dialects.

PAIR WITH Sushi, soft cheeses or caviar with blini. Or drink by itself, as it makes a wonderful aperitif. Serve chilled.

UNCORK Friday nights, Saturday nights, Sundays, Mondays, Wednesdays (of course), and we can't forget Tuesdays or Thursdays.

ALBET I NOYA

Albet i Noya	Petit Albet Brut Cava
WINERY	WINE NAME
Organic Cava	Non-vintage
TYPE	YEAR
Penèdes, Spain	$20
ORIGIN	PRICE	CLOSURE

Cava is the national sparkling wine of Spain, and Albet i Noya makes an outstanding example—and it's organic, too. In fact, the family behind the winery started the process of changing their vineyards to organic production in the 1970s and is now Spain's leading organic wine producer.

As for the Petit Albet Brut, it is dry, but not too dry, with fine bubbles and nutty, toasty, lemony notes. Made with 100 percent handpicked grapes—Xarel-lo, Macabeau and Parellada to be exact—it is an incredible alternative to champagne at a fraction of the cost. Like champagne, however, it is made using the traditional method. That means the wine undergoes its secondary fermentation

(the process that gives it bubbles) in the bottle, not in a tank, as with many inexpensive sparkling wines.

TRIVIA Before being inserted into a bottle, a sparkling wine cork is cylindrical in shape. The cork is compressed when it's inserted into the wine bottle; it develops its distinctive mushroom shape at this stage.

PAIR WITH Oysters, popcorn, sushi. Serve chilled.

UNCORK Baby showers, wedding showers, Christmas, New Year's Eve, any day you need or want bubbles.

BARGAIN BUBBLES

BLU GIOVELLO

Piera Martellozzo	Blu Giovello
WINERY	WINE NAME
Prosecco	Non-vintage
TYPE	YEAR
Treviso, Veneto, Italy	$14
ORIGIN	PRICE

CLOSURE

Winemaker Piera Martellozzo took over the family business from her father in the 1990s and, since then, has been creating a buzz with her fine wines and creative packaging. Blu Giovello—a combination of the Italian words *blu* (the colour of the sea), *giovane* (young) and *bello* (beautiful)—is a label she creates solely for the international market. In other words, they aren't sold in Italy; they're just for people like us Canadians. The blue bottle, with its dragonfly label, is gorgeous, but the wine inside is also fresh and tasty, with crisp lemon, blossom and apple aromas and flavours.

TRIVIA There are more than 5,600 species of dragonflies in the world. At top speed, dragonflies can go more than 50 kilometres (30 miles) per hour. In Indonesia, they are sometimes fried in oil and eaten as a delicacy.

PAIR WITH Sushi, sashimi, soft white cheeses. Not dragonflies. Or just serve (the wine, not dragonflies) as an aperitif. Serve chilled.

UNCORK Now, for weekend picnics, brunches, New Year's Eve, Mother's Day.

DOMAINE COLLIN

Domaine Collin	Cuvée Rosé	
WINERY	WINE NAME	
Crémant de Limoux	Non-vintage	
TYPE	YEAR	
Limoux, Languedoc, France	$22	
ORIGIN	PRICE	CLOSURE

Philippe Collin grew up in a Champagne family, but insanely-expensive land prices in the region forced him to start his own winery dream elsewhere. He chose Limoux, a small region in Languedoc in southern France. Now he makes brilliant sparkling wines in the traditional method, the same way they make them in Champagne. This blend of Chardonnay with a splash of Pinot Noir has the most beautiful tiny bubbles that release delicate aromas of cherry, brioche, strawberry, pear and a bit of smoke. It's just lovely, and the tart acidity makes it an ideal wine for all types of foods.

TRIVIA Sparkling wines have been made in Limoux since 1531, the same year that Henry VIII became head of the Church of England.

PAIR WITH Salmon, salads, baked ham, Thai dishes, or serve as an aperitif. Serve chilled.

UNCORK Celebrations, anniversaries, graduations or Tuesday nights (you really can't have too much sparkling wine).

BARGAIN BUBBLES

DR. L SPARKLING RIESLING

Loosen Bros.	Dr. L Sparkling Riesling
WINERY	WINE NAME
Sparkling Riesling	Non-vintage
TYPE	YEAR
Mosel, Germany	$15
ORIGIN	PRICE	CLOSURE

This wine appeared in the 2013 edition of *Uncorked!* An apple a day may keep the doctor away, but when the doctor is this much fun, you'll want him to stick around. The Loosen family has been making wine for more than 200 years, and the winery is still family-owned—rare, in these days of major corporations and multinationals. Two brothers, Ernst and Thomas Loosen, currently head up the winery and its various projects. The Dr. L Sparkling Riesling offers aromas of white peach, flowers and baked pear, and, on the palate, notes of honeycomb and blossom.

TRIVIA Sparkling wine has been made for generations in Germany—where it is often called *sekt*.

PAIR WITH Sushi, light aperitifs, smoked salmon. Serve chilled.

UNCORK Any time there's a doctor in the house, parties (especially those with PhD candidates), weddings, anything.

LA MARCA

La Marca
WINERY

Prosecco
TYPE

Non-vintage
YEAR

Treviso, Veneto, Italy
ORIGIN

$18
PRICE

CLOSURE

This wine appeared in the 2013 edition of *Uncorked!* Good packaging doesn't always mean good wine, but really, these bargain bubbles are both—a fancy-looking label and a fancy taste, too. They're fresh and clean-tasting, with notes of honey, grapefruit and just a touch of toast. Created more than 40 years ago, the winery gets its name from La Marca Trevigiana, the heart of Italy's Prosecco region. La Marca's Fabrizio Gatto began his winemaking career at the age of 14

(yes, you read that correctly) when he was accepted into the Conegliano Veneto School of Enology. Like every Prosecco, it's made from 100 percent Glera grapes.

TRIVIA More than just stylish wine comes from Treviso; the clothing company Benetton was also founded in the northern Italian city.

PAIR WITH Seafood in garlic butter, smoked salmon, sushi, white fish dishes. Or just enjoy it as an aperitif. Serve chilled.

UNCORK Any time, any place, especially if we are coming for dinner.

MONTEVICOR

Pagos Familia Langa	Montevicor	
WINERY	WINE NAME	
Cava	Non-vintage	
TYPE	YEAR	
Calatayud, Spain	$21	
ORIGIN	PRICE	CLOSURE

The Langa family has produced wines at this Spanish estate since the 1860s. The latest generation to handle the grapes, brothers Juan and Cesar Langa Gonzalez, make still red wines as well as cavas. This blend of Chardonnay and Macabeo (a grape often used in Spanish sparkling wines) has great balance and flavours of apple cobbler, green apple, pear, spice, toast and a bit of raspberry.

TRIVIA While most Cavas are produced around Penedès in the northeastern part of the country, they can be made pretty much anywhere in Spain.

PAIR WITH Ginger beef, tapas fish dishes, creamy pastas, roast chicken. Serve chilled.

UNCORK With takeout dinners, baby showers, Christmas, New Year's Eve, summer brunches.

PRONTO

Paola Rinaldini Viticoltore	Pronto	
WINERY	WINE NAME	
Lambrusco	Non-vintage	
TYPE	YEAR	
Emilia-Romagna, Italy	$19	
ORIGIN	PRICE	CLOSURE

If you were of legal drinking age in the 1970s and early 1980s, you may cringe at the thought of drinking Lambrusco because you remember the sweet, fizzy alco-pop that was such a hit then.

But true Lambrusco, as Italians will tell you, is the dry sparkling wine of Northern Italy's Emilia-Romagna region, where prosciutto, Parmigiano Reggiano and true balsamic vinegar come from. Expect mild ("frizzante" is the term) bubbles and a dark purple colour, with delicate notes of graphite, cocoa powder and berries. The grapes? A blend of Salamino, Marani and Ancellotta, three of the four legal Lambrusco grapes.

TRIVIA The name "Pronto" comes from the way so many Italians answer the phone: they say "pronto" the way we say "hello."

PAIR WITH Charcuterie (especially prosciutto), Parmigiano Reggiano drizzled with real balsamic vinegar. Serve chilled.

UNCORK Now, with wine geeks, Italophiles and real Italians.

BARGAIN BUBBLES

SEGURA VIUDAS

Segura Viudas	Brut Reserva	
WINERY	WINE NAME	
Cava	Non-vintage	
TYPE	YEAR	
Penèdes, Spain	$18	
ORIGIN	PRICE	CLOSURE

UNCORKED!

This wine has appeared in every edition of *Uncorked!* This is a perennial favourite, and with good reason. Sigura Viudas, based on an estate constructed in the 11th century, consistently produces wines of quality at great prices. Ideal for festive occasions, the first sip will bring flavours of green apple, white peach, smoke, toast, pear, lemon and lime. The depth of flavour and acidity gives this wine the stuffing to pair with a range of foods. Like most cavas, it's made from three Spanish grapes: Macabeo, Parellada and Xarel-lo.

TRIVIA "Segura Viudas" translates to "safe widow."

PAIR WITH Eggs Benedict, white fish dishes, pastas with creamy sauces, grilled shrimp, or on its own. Serve chilled.

UNCORK Birthdays, New Year's Eve, the end of exams, celebrating a promotion.

TWO OCEANS

Two Oceans	Sauvignon Blanc Brut
WINERY	WINE NAME
Sparkling wine	2012
TYPE	YEAR
Western Cape, South Africa	$13
ORIGIN	PRICE

CLOSURE

This is the wine to open when you're making mimosas (sparkling wine and orange juice) or you want to teach your entire book club how to "sabre" a bottle of bubbles (make sure the wine is very, very cold before attempting it!). Two Oceans gets its name from the fact that it's made where the Atlantic and Indian oceans meet. The wine itself is very pale, almost clear, with big, zesty, crisp bubbles and pleasant lemon and lime aromas and flavours.

TRIVIA The Indian Ocean is the world's third-largest ocean. The Atlantic is the world's second-largest ocean, although the ancient Greeks believed it was one great river that flowed around the world.

PAIR WITH Brunch dishes, calamari, salmon, sushi. Serve chilled.

UNCORK Now, with good friends, book club gatherings, or any time you need reliable bubbles for cocktails.

BARGAIN BUBBLES

VALDO

Valdo	Marca Oro
WINERY	WINE NAME
Prosecco	Non-vintage
TYPE	YEAR
Veneto, Italy	$19
ORIGIN	PRICE	CLOSURE

Like most Proseccos and many other sparkling wines not made in Champagne, France, the Valdo Marca Oro is made by what winemakers call the tank method or "charmat" (pronounced *shar-MAT*). The sparkling wine undergoes its secondary fermentation (which creates the bubbles) in a tank, not in the bottle. Marca Oro—literally, the "gold mark"—features pretty notes of green apple, pear, spice, and maybe a hint of cherry.

TRIVIA The Veneto region includes two of Italy's most famous cities, Venice (canals and gondolas) and Verona (where Shakespeare's Romeo and Juliet lived out their short, star-crossed lives).

PAIR WITH Sushi, popcorn, calamari, smoked salmon. Serve chilled.

UNCORK Now, for New Year's Eve, Fridays, any time you want an instant party.

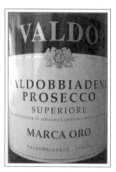

ZARDETTO

Zardetto	Z
WINERY	WINE NAME
Prosecco	Non-vintage
TYPE	YEAR
Treviso, Veneto, Italy	$21
ORIGIN	PRICE

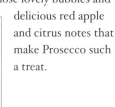 CLOSURE

Behind this Prosecco-maker's family are some fascinating stories. Almost 100 years ago, Bepi Zardetto lost his horse and cart—which was loaded with wine barrels—at the Battle of Caporetto during the First World War. The terrible battle took place on the Austrian–Italian front, in what is now part of Slovenia, and more than 10,000 Italians died. Even now, the term "Caporetto" is sometimes used in Italian to refer to a major defeat. Luckily for us, however, Zardetto survived, and his descendants continue to make wines such as this one. Expect those lovely bubbles and

delicious red apple and citrus notes that make Prosecco such a treat.

TRIVIA Thinking of going to Italy? The Prosecco Road is a narrow, winding road, about 64 kilometres (40 miles) long, that winds its way through the heart of the region.

PAIR WITH Popcorn, sushi, sashimi, calamari. Serve chilled.

UNCORK Now, at brunch, New Year's Eve, first dates and last-minute parties.

ZINCK

Domaine Zinck	Crémant d'Alsace Brut
WINERY	WINE NAME
Crémant	Non-vintage
TYPE	YEAR
Alsace, France	$22
ORIGIN	PRICE	CLOSURE

This wine appeared in the first edition of *Uncorked!* I just love the label on this traditional-method sparkler from France's Alsace region. The silhouette of a person with butterfly wings set against a tangerine background kind of looks like a scene from the opening credits of a James Bond movie. You won't find Daniel Craig here, though. The real stars are Pinot Blanc, Pinot Noir and Chardonnay. Look for green apple, pear, spice and white peach flavours, plus a little bit of smoke and blossom on the nose.

TRIVIA "Crémant" is the name given to a group of French sparkling wines that are made in the same way as champagne, but don't come from the prestigious region. Crémants are made all around the country, including Burgundy, Alsace and the Loire Valley.

PAIR WITH Desserts like apple pie or peach cobbler, citrus salads, stir-fries. Serve chilled.

UNCORK Summer solstice, James Bond movie nights (not everyone can afford the bubbles that 007 drinks), Friday nights after work.

SWEET & FORTIFIED WINES

BRICCO QUAGLIA

La Spinetta	Bricco Quaglia	
WINERY	WINE NAME	
Sweet sparkling wine	2012	
TYPE	YEAR	
Moscato d'Asti, Piedmont, Italy	$22	
ORIGIN	PRICE	CLOSURE

La Spinetta is one of Italy's most famous wineries. Located in Piedmont, close to the mountains in the nation's northwest, La Spinetta produces complex—and tannic—red wines from the Nebbiolo grape. But the first wine La Spinetta ever produced was Moscato d'Asti. This version is wonderfully light and fresh, with soft bubbles and a rich sweetness. You'll find flavours of apricot, peach, raisin, honey and blossom. A streak of mineral comes in on the finish, keeping the sweetness in balance. It's so good, you might want to buy two bottles. And it's only 5.5 percent alcohol, to boot.

TRIVIA The Bricco Quaglia was the first single-vineyard-designated Moscato d'Asti produced in Italy. That means all the Muscat grapes come from the same vineyard.

PAIR WITH Light desserts, Sunday brunch, or on its own. Serve chilled.

UNCORK Mother's Day, hot summer afternoons, picnics, baby showers.

UNCORKED!

ERRAZURIZ

Errazuriz	Late Harvest Sauvignon Blanc
WINERY	WINE NAME
Sauvignon Blanc	2011
TYPE	YEAR
Casablanca Valley, Chile	$14 for 375 mL
ORIGIN	PRICE · CLOSURE

An earlier vintage of this wine appeared in the 2010 edition of *Uncorked!* This cheerful sweetie costs considerably less than icewine, yet gives a similar sweet kick at the end of a meal. The same family has owned the winery for more than 130 years. President Eduardo Chadwick is a direct descendent of Don Maximiano Errázuriz, who started the winery in the Aconcagua Valley; the family now owns property in many of Chile's top wine-producing regions. As for the wine, expect notes of warm lemon, ripe passion fruit, pineapple, tangerine, honey and flowers.

TRIVIA Don Maximiano Errázuriz, the winery's founder, was a famous (and wealthy) Chilean politician who owned a copper mining company. At one point, he backed up his government by lending it money. His own money.

PAIR WITH Plain pound cake, angel food cake, flan topped with fresh mango or berries. Or serve by itself in tiny glasses.

UNCORK Now, as a celebratory drink at the end of a fancy dinner.

NUTTY SOLERA

Gonzalez Byass	Nutty Solera
WINERY	WINE NAME

Sherry	Non-vintage
TYPE	YEAR

Jerez, Spain	$16	
ORIGIN	PRICE	CLOSURE

Gonzalez Byass started in 1885 when Manuel Maria González Ángel, who was making sherry in Jerez, joined forces with Robert Blake Byass, his agent in England. More than 100 years later, the portfolio now includes still wines, sparkling wines, brandies and liqueurs. This sherry was made using the solera system, a method of blending and aging wine that mixes young wines with older wines. (That's why you don't see vintages on solera wines.)

This sherry is an Oloroso, meaning it was exposed to oxygen, which gives it unique savoury flavours and a darker orange-brown colour. The flavours include walnut, orange peel, clove, cinnamon and dried apricot. Off-dry, with a long finish, it is a great way to introduce yourself to an interesting style of fortified wine.

TRIVIA Sherry, which is produced at the southern tip of Spain, near Gibraltar, is believed to have been developed after the Moors introduced distillation to the Iberian Peninsula around AD 700.

PAIR WITH Red meat and game, nuts, desserts, dried fruits, or enjoy on its own.

UNCORK Winter dinner parties, weekday contemplation, or with curious wine geeks.

WARRE'S WARRIOR

Warre's	Warrior
WINERY	WINE NAME
Port	Non-vintage
TYPE	YEAR
Douro Valley, Portugal	$16 for 375 mL
ORIGIN	PRICE

CLOSURE

Warrior is, according to legendary producer Warre's, the oldest brand of port in the world. It has been shipped from northern Portugal since the 1750s. Port is made by adding grape spirit—kind of like a vodka made from grapes—to a batch of fermenting red wine. The high alcohol of the grape spirit kills the yeast that was fermenting the grapes. Since the fermentation was stopped early, there's still a lot of sugar left in the wine, and that's why port is sweet. The Warrior has flavours that include spice, blueberry, molasses, vanilla, toast, raspberry and cherry.

TRIVIA Brits became interested in wines from Portugal when wars with France made it difficult to get French wine. But when still wines were shipped from Portugal to Britain, the long journey often led to spoiled wines. Then someone discovered that if the wine was fortified with alcohol, it wasn't spoiled and, in fact, it was delicious. Port, named after Oporto—the Portuguese city it is shipped from—was born.

PAIR WITH Blue cheeses like Gorgonzola or roquefort, nutty or chocolate desserts, or on its own.

UNCORK After holiday dinners, unwinding after work, reading on a cold winter afternoon, while planning warm European holidays.

FIFTEEN FABULOUS FINDS FOR $15 OR LESS

While all the wines in this guide are worth trying, if you're looking to get extra bang for fewer bucks, check out this list of some of our favourite wines that sell for south of $15.

1. Intis, Finca Las Moras, Sauvignon Blanc, 2011 (San Juan, Argentina) $9

2. La Puerta, Valle de la Puerta, Torrontés, 2011 (Famatina Valley, Argentina) $11

3. Castillo de Monséran, Garnacha, 2010 (Cariñena, Spain) $11

4. Green Label, Deinhard, Riesling, 2010 (Mosel, Germany) $12

5. 120, Santa Rita, Cabernet Sauvignon, 2011 (Central Valley, Chile) $12

6. Santa Julia, Bodega Santa Julia, Malbec, 2011 (Mendoza, Argentina) $12

7. Verano, Shiraz, 2011 (Valencia, Spain) $12

8. The Wolftrap, Boekenhoutskloof, Viognier/Chenin Blanc/Grenache Blanc, 2011 (Western Cape, South Africa) $13

9. El Petit Bonhomme, Nathalie Bonhomme, Monastrell/Garnacha/Syrah, 2011 (Jumilla, Spain) $13

10. Castaño Old Vines, Monastrell/Mourvèdre, 2011 (Yecla, Spain) $13

11. Two Oceans, Sauvignon Blanc Brut, Sparkling wine, 2012 (Western Cape, South Africa) $13

12. 1884 Reservado, Bodegas Escorihuela, Cabernet Sauvignon, 2011 (Mendoza, Argentina) $14

13. Bila-Haut, M. Chapoutier, Syrah/Grenache/Carignan, 2011 (Côtes du Roussillon Villages, France) $14

14. Kaiken, Malbec, 2010 (Mendoza, Argentina) $14

15. Galil Mountain, Rosé, Sangiovese/Barbera/Pinot Noir/Syrah, 2011 (Upper Galilee, Israel) $14

WHERE TO BUY THESE WINES

Many of these wines are available at wine shops across the province. If you're looking for a particular label, however, and you can't find it, try the following:

GO TO ALBERTA-LIQUOR-GUIDE.COM.

This site is run by the Alberta government, and you can search to find the name of the importer and, in most cases, individual stores that carry or have carried the product. Call to ensure stock before you show up and demand a case.

CHECK OUT SOME OF THE ONLINE SHOPPING SITES.

At least two, zyn.ca (403-543-8900) and albertawinestein.com (403-475-8189), can ship wines across the province. Others, such as kensingtonwinemarket.com (1-888-283-9004) and highlanderwine.com (403-777-1922), can ship within Calgary.

FURTHER RESOURCES

READ A BOOK

Want to know more about wine? There are dozens of great books out there that will inspire you and further your wine knowledge. Here are a few of our favourites.

Any of the Dummies guides for wine lovers, especially *Pairing Food and Wine for Dummies* by Canadian Master Sommelier John Szabo, and the ones by Ed McCarthy, including *Wine for Dummies* and *Red Wine for Dummies* (John Wiley and Sons)

Discovering Wine: A Refreshingly Unfussy Beginner's Guide to Finding, Tasting, Judging, Storing, Serving, Cellaring and, Most of All, Discovering Wine by Joanna Simon (Simon & Schuster)

Kevin Zraly's Windows on the World Complete Wine Course (Sterling Publishing)

The Oxford Companion to Wine, edited by Jancis Robinson (Oxford University Press)

Tony Aspler's Cellar Book: How to Design, Build, Stock and Manage Your Wine Cellar Wherever You Live (Random House Canada)

Wine Grapes: A Complete Guide to 1,368 Vine Varieties, Including Their Origins and Flavours by Jancis Robinson, Julia Harding and José Vouillamoz (Ecco)

The World Atlas of Wine, by Hugh Johnson and Jancis Robinson (Mitchell Beazley)

TAKE A CLASS

Most large wine stores offer tastings and seminars, or ask the sommeliers at your favourite local restaurants if they host winemakers' dinners. Or check out a wine organization:

- The Wine & Spirit Education Trust (WSET, west.co.uk) offers courses around the world, including in Calgary, and if you pass the exam at the end, you'll achieve international certification—handy, in case you ever need to impress, oh, say, a cute single person at a wine bar on the other side of the world. Both Darren and Shelley hold Level 3 Advanced WSET certification, but we aren't confessing if we've ever used it to impress people on the other side of the world.

- The International Sommelier Guild (internationalsommelier.com) is another globally recognized certificate program. Like the WSET, there are different levels. Take just one, or work your way to the top.

- The European Wine Academy (europeanwineacademy.org) offers courses in English for beginners, professionals and wannabe professionals. Some of the courses are offered online, so it doesn't matter where you live.

ACKNOWLEDGEMENTS

THANK YOU—

To Anders, Erik and Steen, who put up with me and a houseful of bottles. To my parents, Phil and Phyllis, who started me on this crazy, wine-soaked journey and who have always shared their favourite deals with me. To all my aunts and uncles and cousins who bought the last two books and told all of their friends—I love you! To my brother, Doug, and to Shirley, Mike and Annette, Darren and Terri, Hildur and Alex, Alison and Don, Val and Robert, Chris and Leonie, Harry and Dianne, Aviv and Michal, Kevin and Mairi, for dinners, wine and endless conversations about wine. To my friends in the wine industry in Canada and beyond, for generously sharing samples and suggestions, and for answering my never-ending questions. To my friends and colleagues at the *Calgary Herald* (especially Val Berenyi) and the now-defunct *Wine Access,* for your patience, editing skills and tasting tips. To Jim and the folks at *Domus* magazine, and Kathy and Gail at *City Palate,* and CBC Radio, especially Russell Bowers. And to the wonderful folks at Whitecap, for making the third book as much fun as the first.

—Shelley

First, I have to thank Shelley for including me in this wonderful and rewarding project. Also, to my wife, Terri, thanks so much for your support and understanding during a hectic period of tasting, writing, staring out the window, mumbling, and writing some more. You're a terrific proofreader as well! Also a big thanks to friends and wine adventure co-conspirators Colleen and Colin, for your lively input. As well, to fellow WSET grad Mairi, thanks for bringing fresh energy to the slog. To my friends from *Wine Access,* Tom, Amanda, Laura, Kathy, Keiron and Tony, thanks for sharing your insights and good cheer. As well, I would never have reached this point without the trust and support of so many friends at the *Calgary Herald,* particularly Lorne, Monica, Paul, Steve, Chris and Tom. To the scores of agents who submitted bottles, thanks for taking the time out of your hectic schedules. To the folks at Whitecap, thanks for including me on this journey. And finally, a huge thanks to my parents, Gladys and Walter, and my sisters, Diane and Patti, and their families, as well as Terri's family, parents Ron and Doris, sister Pam and brother Jody and their families. I would like to dedicate this book to Walter and Ron, who both passed away during its writing. You were passionate about wine and life, and you are greatly missed.

—Darren

INDEX

Want to know how to use this index? Look for wines under the winery name (this is followed by the specific wine name, if there is any, for example, Crew Wine Company 'Matchbook').

Also look for wines under a grape category ("Cabernet Sauvignon", for example) or wine type ("sparkling wine", for example), or under "red blends", "white blends" or "organic wines". If you're looking for wines from a specific country or region, go back to the table of contents at the front of the book and go to the region you're interested in from there. Can't find what you're looking for? Bust out and try something new. You may be pleasantly surprised.

INDEX

UNCORKED!

UNCORKED!

ABOUT THE AUTHORS

Born and raised in Alberta, **Shelley Boettcher** once had a psychic tell her she'd make a good used-car salesman. Instead she became a writer, after stints as a cook, a chambermaid, a nanny and the only woman on a rural construction crew. Based in Calgary, she is an award-winning writer whose work has appeared in newspapers and magazines around the world. She is a national wine columnist for CBC Radio's morning weekend shows, and a wine columnist for *Domus* magazine. She wrote the first two editions of *Uncorked!* (2010 and 2012). She's also the former executive editor of *Wine Access,* a now-defunct national wine magazine, and the former wine columnist for the *Calgary Herald*. She holds a master's degree in journalism from the University of Western Ontario, and advanced certification from the Wine and Spirits Education Trust. Follow her on Twitter @shelley_wine and become a friend of this book on Facebook by searching for "Uncorked." She also blogs at www.shelleyboettcher.com.

Darren Oleksyn got an early, hands-on introduction to the wine world by helping his father craft homemade fruit wines out of raspberries, chokecherries, tomatoes, and once, even grapes. From the small farming community of Kelliher, Saskatchewan, he has worked as a journalist for 20 years, copy editing and covering the sports, news and business beats at the *Prince Albert Daily-Herald* and *Regina Leader-Post* before moving to the *Calgary Herald* in 2004. Always interested in wine, his passion hit a new level in Calgary thanks to the wide product selection, the numerous wine events and the knowledge of wine-loving workers in the city's boutique stores. That led to wine classes and visits to wineries in British Columbia, Ontario, California, Oregon, Arizona, Italy, Portugal and Germany. He started writing about wine in 2011 when he joined *Wine Access* magazine as managing editor. A holder of the Wine and Spirits Education Trust Level 3 Advanced certificate, he now writes a monthly wine column for the *Calgary Herald*. Follow him on Twitter @doleksyn.